1.

THE I.C.I AFFAIR

One of the most sensational
murder mysteries ever to sweep
British society

by

R.M.Bevan

1926

The I.C.I. Affair
One of the most sensational
murder mysteries ever to sweep
British society

Edited & adapted from 'The I.C.I Affair' (2017)

Copyright © 2022 R.M.Bevan & Cheshire Country Publishing. The right of R.M.Bevan to be identified as the author of this work has been asserted by him in accordance with the Copyright, Designs and Patents Act, 1988.

No part of this book may be reproduced or transmitted in any form or by any means, electronic or mechanical, including photocopying, recording or any information storage or retrieval system, without prior permission in writing from the Publisher.

ISBN
978-0-949001-70-2

*CHESHIRE COUNTRY PUBLISHING,
MARTINS LANE, HARGRAVE, CHESTER, CH3 7RX
TEL: 01829 741651. EMAIL: editor@cc-publishing.co.uk
WEBSITE: http://www.cc-publishing.co.uk*

FOREWORD

NEVER has there been a year quite like 1926 and those who lived through it would not forget the General Strike, the ceaseless months of bitter industrial conflict, the nation brought to the cusp of anarchy. The trade unions and government fought a pitch-battle of wills until, in early November, the red flag of dispirited mineworkers finally gave way to the tarnished white of surrender. Sensing 'Peace in the coalfields', the newspaper headlines vied with even more sensational news, a compelling mystery that would stun the highest echelons of business and society.

At the heart of the matter was the formation of Imperial Chemical Industries, what would come to be a vast commercial icon of the 20th century. I.C.I.'s history is well documented, history as it were written by the victors, but far less recorded, and certainly less well known, is a story of betrayal, murder and suicide at the very moment of the company's astonishingly swift founding in 1926.

Locked in conflict were two enormously egotistical individuals. One, Sir Alfred Mond, was an international financier and major political figure who had once knocked on the door of greatness. The other, a vivacious, unpredictable authoress who aspired to the highest rungs of social position and whose murder, in different circumstances, would have made her a cause célèbre in the mythology of crime. Between them stood loyal, stoical Roscoe Brunner, a highly respected industrialist who turned to his revolver to ensure an enigmatic secret went with him to the grave.

In 2003 I published an initial investigation into the I.C.I. mystery and during the intervening years much additional information has come to light, not least due to modern technology and the instant availability of otherwise obscure records. Publication itself also flushed out additional fascinating material of which I was not aware. Even so, I certainly did not intend to re-write, or adapt, the original, i.e. until, quite unexpectedly, I received a full-page 1930s' feature from the London Evening Standard resurrecting what it declared to be 'The most sensational case ever to sweep British society'. 'What was the secret – What do you think?' implored the headlines.

Intriguingly, the Evening Standard also suggested there was far more to the affair than had ever surfaced and this too remains my long-held belief, that an extraordinary cover-up masked the Brunner deaths in order to protect the embryonic foundations of I.C.I..

Power, wealth and influence were brought to bear and I trust this final revision convinces the doubters, those who may still believe the truth was not buried, that the tragedy, as the official investigation concluded, was personal, a collateral, but incidental, consequence to the founding of I.C.I..

R.M.Bevan

In October 1926, Roscoe Brunner learned that he was not one of the twelve names put forward for the Board of the proposed new I.C.I. Hurt as he was it was nothing to the fury of his wife who set about making a public issue of the slight. On 3 November 1926 he shot her and then shot himself.

*The official version from
'A hundred years of Alkali in Cheshire'.*

Chapter 1

IN the fashionable London suburb of Roehampton curtains were drawn against the year's first winter blast. Away in the distance fireworks flared into the night sky as the clock of Holy Trinity Church commenced to strike ten. At the junction of Medfield Street and Roehampton Lane, a young policeman engaged on mundane traffic duty was suddenly roused by the shouts of a panic-stricken woman running towards him. 'Come quickly,' she cried, 'Something terrible has happened'. A few minutes later PC Thomas Whitwell was gazing at two lifeless bodies in a pool of blood on a bedroom floor. One, apparently the lady of the house, had been shot through the neck at close range; the other, her husband, had died from a single bullet to the temple. He still clasped in his hand a tiny revolver.

PC Whitwell immediately sealed off the bedroom and from the house telephone contacted his superiors at Wandsworth police station. Detectives were on the scene within half an hour and though no-one had heard shots or an argument, detectives quickly came to the conclusion it was a straightforward 'domestic'. The man had murdered his wife and then shot himself.

What the police did not appreciate was they had on their hands a national sensation. On the following morning, Thursday November 4, 1926, the Roehampton deaths were briefly reported on the wireless, but it was the London evening newspapers that brought home the first detailed account of the unexplained demise of wealthy industrialist Roscoe Brunner and his Irish authoress wife, Ethel. The public was electrified and, as the story began to unfold, the question on everybody's lips was Why? Why had Roscoe and Ethel Brunner, affluent and successful beyond the dreams of ordinary mortals, died in such violent circumstances? Were they not the perfect couple blessed with everything to live for? They socialised in the highest circles, employed a staff of servants, a chauffeur to drive their limousine, and they had recently taken possession of a grand London mansion. Moreover they were parents to two fine sons approaching manhood and their daughter was married into European royalty. In short, the sun appeared to perpetually shine on the Brunners.

Tagged by the newspapers as the 'Roehampton Mystery' reports were soon flashing across the globe for publication in newspapers from Buenos Aires to Bombay, Singapore to Sydney, New York to Hong Kong. Little was left to the imagination and by the weekend all of Fleet Street was of one steadfast opinion, that Roscoe Brunner, a sick man, had been driven to murder by his wife's interference in business affairs connected with his failure to secure a seat on the inaugural board of directors of Imperial Chemical Industries (I.C.I.), a vast company in the process of being established at lightning speed. The Daily Mail reported: 'Although Mr Brunner felt the change in his fortunes, his wife took it even more to heart. She felt the alteration in her husband's commercial eminence so much that it

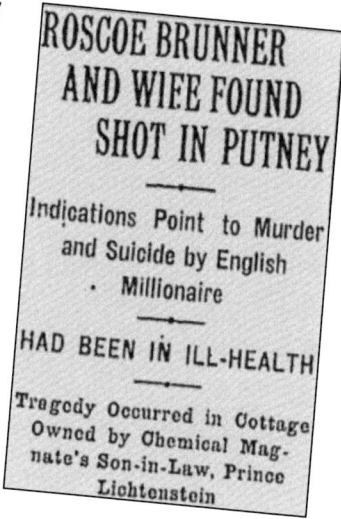

> **ROSCOE BRUNNER AND WIFE FOUND SHOT IN PUTNEY**
>
> Indications Point to Murder and Suicide by English Millionaire
>
> **HAD BEEN IN ILL-HEALTH**
>
> Tragedy Occurred in Cottage Owned by Chemical Magnate's Son-in-Law, Prince Lichtenstein

obsessed her. He tried to pacify her, but apparently without success, and then came the formation of Imperial Chemical Industries, but there is to be no place for Roscoe Brunner on the new board of directors. He has been snubbed and his wife was known to be furious. She said he had not been treated fairly and, letting her anger get the better of her discretion, she made a round of visits to influential people with the object of trying to get her husband's grievances redressed. She visited people at their private houses, and at one, it is alleged, an unpleasant scene ensued. She went to newspaper offices and tried to arouse interest in her case, evidently moved by a deep-seated sense of grievance that in the constitution of the new board of directors no place had been found for her husband.'

The wildest excesses of the Press were brought into play and one newspaper summing up the Brunners' marriage, declared the couple's former happy relations had snapped and '...there was continual bickering regarding Mrs Brunner's extravagance in the matter of entertainments, dress and other amusements'.

Others, not least the Daily Express, described Ethel Brunner as a 'highly-strung, temperamental woman' who had tried to dominate her husband. Another, perhaps delivering the coup de grâce in an avalanche of salacious gossip, revealed that six months earlier a celebrated West End clairvoyant had warned her 'good friend' Mrs Brunner she had seen in crystal that she was destined to meet a violent death. It was compulsive reading, no matter from what dubious sources the reports emanated.

'Terrible tragedy in London', 'Secret of shot millionaire', 'Tragic quarrel over combine', 'A misguided wife', 'Secrets of mansion tragedy', 'A wife's indiscretions', 'Impulsive Lady Bountiful', 'Drama of high finance', '...the apparent eclipse of a magnate from his former eminent position'.

The Press coverage knew no bounds and at the inquest five days later this was to prove critical. Determined to lance a further frenzy of speculation and innuendo, an incensed coroner chose not to call vital witnesses, or reveal the slightest shred of new evidence beyond that already published in the 1920s' version of the modern tabloids. He complained that the Press coverage, 'misguided and inappropriate', had gone beyond the pale of public decency and if legislation was not forthcoming to neuter the miscreants in their reporting of domestic tragedies, he would, no doubt, have demanded all editors be hanged at Tyburn.

The verdicts – 'murder' of Ethel Brunner and 'suicide whilst of unsound mind' in the case of Roscoe Brunner – were as merciful as the family could have hoped. The justice system ran its course and, amidst almost paranoid security on the day following the inquest, the two bodies were cremated, committed to the archives, to be buried and forgotten for a hundred years if some had their way.

Chapter 2

THE dead man, Roscoe Brunner, was a leading figure in British industry, an unassuming gentleman who calmly took everything in his stride, the last person imaginable to commit murder. Seldom was a bad word ever spoken of him as, unlike most business leader contemporaries, he possessed a humility that spanned the chasm between workers and management. To say he was well liked is something of an understatement and, when the dreadful news of his death began to filter through, thousands of workers, blue-collar and white-collar, bowed to the memory of their 'Mr Roscoe'. In Cheshire, in his hometown of Northwich, flags draped at half-mast to mark the passing of a caring employer, benefactor and a pillar of the community who, until a few months before his death, had been the patriarchal chairman of Brunner Mond & Company, one of Britain's foremost chemical manufacturers.

Roscoe Brunner's wife, Ethel, was of a different cut, headstrong, tempestuous and, certainly, a woman full of her own self-importance. As one household servant later put it: 'Not everyone's cup of tea'. At the height of his career Roscoe Brunner had been the chairman of an international business with 50,000 employees worldwide, and whenever it suited his wife's purpose she brazenly traded on his position and wealth. A striking-looking woman, said to be 'rather tall with ashen-gold hair', she was not universally popular but her charity work, her support of good causes and tireless efforts on behalf of her chosen political party, had few equals in Cheshire and it was not without reason that she was known as 'Lady Bountiful'. Her life revolved around the most fashionable Continental resorts, lavish entertainment, the opening of fetes and bazaars, serving on committees, organising her inferiors and distributing largesse, something that did not always go down well with the established, well-heeled ladies of Cheshire's muck and manure set who, jealous of 'new industrial money', complained she lacked breeding.

This latter barb, bitchily imparted due to Ethel Brunner being of Irish descent and, therefore, an interloper, 'not one of us', was well wide of the mark. If the county ladies had bothered to check they would have discovered her upbringing, in Dublin and London, probably far exceeded their own. The eldest of three daughters to Dr. Arthur Houston QC she had learned from her father the ways of justice, fairness and a determination to seek the best station in life. Her mother had nurtured an interest in music and theatre and, during her formative years, the two were inseparable on the sophisticated London circuit. To crown it all Ethel was presented as a debutante to the future Queen Alexandra.

Whether she found a suitor at the 'Coming Out' Ball is not recorded, but in any event a marital match was already in the minds of her parents who were close friends to Roscoe Brunner's father, a Liberal politician who had co-founded the Brunner Mond chemical company, an enterprise that by the end of the 19th century was almost giving him licence to print money. Dashing and genial Roscoe was about to become the hands-on, day-to-day manager of the business, his father's heir-apparent and, therefore, a 'good catch' in every sense. In return Roscoe was captivated by Ethel Houston's beauty and the mystique of Irishness, although he knew full well she was never likely to be the archetypal Victorian wife, languid at her needlework, simpering fetchingly at his side.

Romance blossomed and by the time of Roscoe and Ethel's marriage at the end of the 19th century the entire British heavy chemical industry was in the hands of forty or fifty manufacturers whose works were predominantly located around the saltfields of Cheshire and the neighbouring parts of Lancashire. Brunner Mond & Company stood at the head, the most prosperous of all. Thirty years before on the winds of Victorian entrepreneurism Roscoe's father had launched the company with Ludwig Mond, a gifted German Jewish scientist. They were both senior employees at a large firm in the town of Widnes, a once marshy hamlet that had been transformed into an abomination of the Industrial Revolution. Visitors to the district often wondered how life could be sustained in this 'foul air and blackened landscape' where the human misery in the back-to-back houses of the labouring classes was said to be matched only by the sinuous-streaked waters of the River Mersey.

John Brunner and Ludwig Mond resided with their families in middle-class surrounds high above Widnes. Brunner and his wife, Salome, had three daughters and three sons, John (Jack), Sydney and Roscoe, whilst nearby, Mond and his wife Frida were parents to sons Robert and Alfred. The two families were inseparable and John Brunner and Ludwig Mond were soon feverishly discussing plans to set up in business on their own account. What they had in mind was a pioneering chemical works to manufacture soda ash, a primary raw material in the expanding glass, soap, paper and textile industries. The key was an affordable site upon which to build their chemical plant and they were drawn towards the town of Northwich at the centre of the salt industry. Northwich, though not half as appalling as Widnes, was still described at the time as a 'smoking hell hole, like a house on fire'. The would-be partners were undeterred and turned their attention to the outskirts of the town, pleasant tree-lined countryside on the banks of the River Weaver, a tributary of the Mersey. The location was perfect for their requirements, too perfect, in fact, and, hypocritically, the powerful local gentry, many of whom had grown fat from the salt-producing hell hole, stood shoulder to shoulder in abhorrence and denial. Brunner and Mond could build their stinking chemical works anywhere, but not in these sacred precincts.

They raged that the neighbouring chemical industry of Widnes, was a horror, with belching thick black smoke day and night, a nauseating odour of rotten eggs and dumped chemical waste. In the drawing rooms of the exalted there was talk of floggings and the setting of dogs on the miscreants and to make matters worse, Mond was a foreigner, and his rather fearsome appearance and his Continental manner hardened the county prejudice. He was about 5ft-8ins tall, slightly stooped and always wore a black broad-brimmed, shapeless hat which half concealed a heavily bearded face, powerful racial nose and a much tortured and disfigured left eye, a lasting testimony to a chemical experiment.

With the spirit of Agincourt running through their veins the Cheshire nobility schemed and conspired to deprive Brunner and Mond of the land they so desperately needed until, finally, they came upon 130 acres of land attached to Winnington Hall, a Georgian mansion on the outskirts of Northwich and a most unlikely setting for a monstrous chemical works. Winnington Hall had previously been a ladies' finishing school or, as the headmistress put it, '...a school for the daughters of the gently born' whose visiting luminaries included John Ruskin and Charles Halle. Winnington Hall had greatly appealed to Ruskin's sensibilities and he wrote to his father: 'This is such a fine place I shall stay till Monday. The house stands in a superb park, full of trees and sloping down to the river. I like Mr Halle so very much. He was very happy yesterday evening, and actually played quadrilles for us to dance to...'

Literature and music were of no concern to John Brunner and Ludwig Mond when they opened negotiations to purchase the Winnington estate, the best site in all England for their chemical works. They required only a portion of the land, but it was all or nothing and, in the end, they had to mortgage themselves to the hilt, so leaving themselves vastly under-capitalised and halfway through their second year of production they had nothing left but their credit.

To make matters worse, immense technical problems arose. Everything that could break down, did break down, and Ludwig Mond, his cigar puffing vigorously in his mouth, became a tyrant as he cursed and spurred on workers. 'Heaven help the man who does his best and fails – for then there is no hope for him and I've no use for him,' he stormed. The uncertainty in those first years was unrelenting, but, amidst the growing chimneys and skeleton towers, they moved their families into Winnington Hall.

When the great adventure began Ludwig Mond's youngest son, Alfred, was still a few months short of his fifth birthday, but robust and blunt he was similar in character to his father and a clash of like-temperaments dominated his childhood. It was said that Alfred came to be as suppressed as any hard-bitten worker by the fearsome stature and presence of his strong disciplinarian father who frowned upon him as something of a family fool. Just as with his men, Ludwig Mond demanded absolute obedience to his will and he could see only his eldest son, Robert, pursuing a worthwhile scientific career. The Mond boys were raised in the strict enclave of a typical 19th century family, typical that is in as far as Ludwig and Frida Mond remained staunchly German all of their lives and insisted upon their sons being attended by a German governess. The Monds despised Provincial England and when at home Alfred and his brother were permitted only to speak German. Even their books and play things were acquired from Germany and when it came to them attending weekly boarding school they were sent to an establishment run by a Mr Schelling, a hard and cold Prussian headmaster.

In the other wing of Winnington Hall, John Brunner doted on his children and amongst his large family he was able to relax away from the chronic difficulties that, more than once, saw the business on the verge of bankruptcy. Personal tragedy was also to impinge upon John Brunner when his business acumen was more critically required than ever before. In the summer of 1874, six children in nine years' of marriage an exacting toll, his wife Salome died. The Brunner children were whisked off to Liverpool, to stay with Salome's parents whilst John Brunner temporarily resided with the Monds. However he sorely missed his family and within a year he married his housekeeper, Ethel Jane Wyman. Ludwig Mond's wife disapproved and tried in vain to keep the Brunner and Mond boys apart, but in the rather surreal world of Winnington they shared rich mischief in the endless steam pipes, furnaces and dark corners. They would steal the men's dinners and hide them, or pelt snow and turf at the office boy and fill the men's hats with lime; they would build dens down by the river and, in winter, skate on the ornamental pond, precious childhood experiences that so bond together men in later life.

By the time the Brunner and Mond boys were entering their teens Winnington had become a much happier place. The size of the plant had doubled, output had trebled and thanks to a combination of John Brunner's resourcefulness and Ludwig Mond's technical skills, each ton of soda ash was beginning to yield a profit.

Ludwig Mond and John Brunner.

The Hollies, Widnes, birthplace of Alfred Mond.

Winnington Hall School.

Winnington Hall in all its former glory.

Winnington Hall later swamped by Brunner Mond.

Chapter 3

THE frustrations of those early years behind them, John Brunner and Ludwig Mond set about incorporating their partnership into a limited company with a market asset value of £800,000. The five sons, destined to be rich men, attended Cheltenham College and then Cambridge University and, with the exception of Alfred Mond, they all did extremely well. Young Mond was never comfortable at either, especially the cloistered confines of Cheltenham where he was distinguished for his foreignness. He could speak German fluently but struggled to correctly pronounce the English language and the situation was no better at Cambridge where he was described as shy, introspective and rather slovenly. A failure as a conventional undergraduate at St John's he excelled only at poker, a dubious talent that landed him the sobriquet 'Beau Mond'. However he was determined that Englishness would not elude him indefinitely and he dreamed of becoming an English gentleman and a politician. 'I shall be the Prime Minister of England,' he vowed.

John Brunner and Ludwig Mond had other ideas, family succession, sons to follow in fathers' footsteps, but it was not to be. Tragedy struck when Sydney Brunner drowned whilst holidaying with the family on Lake Como, and then Jack Brunner and Alfred Mond expressed their determination to pursue careers in politics, Robert Mond in science and archaeology. They took their seats on the board of directors but it was left to Roscoe Brunner, the youngest of the five, to emerge as torch-bearer for the inveterate ambitions of the ageing founders. Self-effacing, easy-going and one of the boys amongst his contemporaries at Cambridge, Roscoe Brunner's heart was always set on a career in industrial management and he spurned the opportunity to be called to the Bar of London's Inner Temple. His father now firmly held the reins of power as chairman of Brunner Mond, although he too had entered politics as a Liberal Member of Parliament and would go on to represent the Northwich constituency for a quarter of a century. Late in life he was elected President of the Liberal Association.

John Brunner fought many fierce political battles but never was he more in the national spotlight than during an early by-election in which he strongly advocated Irish Home Rule. No constituency was seen to be more representative of English society than Northwich and, when Brunner prevailed, the news spread throughout the country and across to Ireland where, said the Manchester Guardian, '... all Dublin was thrown in ecstasy by the Northwich result and the streets of the city rang with the cry of victory'. In the long run the Northwich by-election made little difference to the Irish question and, as history shows, euphoria gave way to bloodshed. However, at a personal level, the election had brought together John Brunner and Dr Arthur Houston who shared the dream of an Irish Free State. Brunner persuaded Houston to enter mainstream British politics and to stand for the Liberals at Warrington. Here Houston went down by a small majority to a local brewer amidst complaints that the town was tied to the beer-barrels as at least sixty-five voters in one ward were allegedly drunk when they voted. Undeterred Brunner and Houston cemented their friendship, shared family holidays and, eventually, brought together Roscoe Brunner and Ethel Houston.

Following their marriage at Paddington in 1898 Roscoe and Ethel set up home at Winnington Hall, by now an incongruous domestic edifice at the centre of Brunner Mond's ugly, sprawling works and a far cry from the genteel way of life the founders had discovered when they had selected the site to establish their chemical plant. Still a fine house Winnington Hall was engulfed by a forest of towers, overhead railways, great steel arches and a thousand windows, and, needless to say, it hardly matched Ethel Brunner's aspirations, especially when she gave birth to their first child, a son, Anthony. Ethel desired somewhere far more fitting, a statement home, spacious and imposing to impress local society who were beginning to pay homage to the huge success of a business over which her husband had become the management figurehead.

A daughter, Shelagh, and a second son, Patrick, added to the family and after much searching Ethel Brunner settled on leasing Belmont Hall, close to Great Budworth, a sleepy, chocolate-box village clustered around an ancient parish church. A mansion of two centuries Belmont Hall included splendid works of art, suites of stately rooms and manicured grounds, just the place for Ethel to flaunt her wealth at dinner parties for over a hundred and soon she was turning on the style, the lady of the manor gazing from her drawing room windows to the far-off belching smoke stacks of Brunner Mond's Winnington Works, the source of her husband's fortune.

Alfred Mond had also taken a bride, Violet Goetze, and Roscoe Brunner stood as best man when they tied the knot. The Goetzes, a London commercial family of Huguenot origin, included Violet's brother, the painter and sculptor Sigismund Goetze. Possessed of an irrepressible charm and an agile mind Violet was the ideal wife to help Alfred Mond achieve his goal. Politics entranced him and with the burgeoning family coffers at his disposal he was more than ever convinced his destiny lay at Westminster. John Brunner, a caring politician who always put constituency and party before personal aspiration, was not so sure about his old partner's son and remarked it was not that he disliked him, he just did not trust him.

Mond had managed to patch-up his Cambridge mistakes at Edinburgh University and he too had qualified for the Bar, but as a barrister on the Chester and North Wales circuit, the stuffiness of chambers bored him and he seized the chance to become Managing Director of Brunner Mond's London office. This was his big break and soon he was a regular visitor to the Houses of Parliament where he began rubbing shoulders with the new young political bloods, including Winston Churchill and David Lloyd George, the fire and brimstone Welsh MP who liked to surround himself with the new Liberal force of 'self-made businessmen'. Mond was hardly that, but he did have access to money, in spades, and Lloyd George was not overly concerned with the subtleties.

Backed by Lloyd George, Mond stood at Salford as Liberal candidate in the 1900 general election but his foreign tongue and his flying of the Temperance flag did him no favours and he performed miserably. It was a mere setback to his long-term ambition of high office and in the 1906 election he was chosen to contest Chester, only twenty miles from Brunner Mond's chemical works. Chester had been a Conservative stronghold for decades and his opponents were quick to lampoon him as a rich Jew, and who had ever heard of a gentleman sending his wife knocking on doors to canvass support? In return the Liberals threw everything at the old Roman town and both Lloyd George and Sir John Brunner (knighted 1895) attended rallies to support their man. In the end the poll could hardly have been closer. The returning officer was about to declare victory for the Conservative candidate when Mond insisted there had been a mistake in the counting. Stepping forward to search bundles of voting papers he found a batch wrongly accredited to his opponent and a recount was ordered. The final margin was so narrow that the single bundle of votes ensured Alfred Mond became the new Member of Parliament for Chester, by just forty-seven votes.

Afterwards, Lloyd George remarked: 'They were afraid of Mond at first, but he stood up before them and the force of his silence was enough to keep them quiet. And then he spoke, with knowledge which was simple and in phrases which were expressive. His sincerity broke down the resentment. They listened to the message of Liberalism. When he was moved by his own thought, he was effective, so much so that you forgot his accent. There were no gestures. His hands were still at his side. There was just the glow of Mond's intelligence – that was all. And yet it was not all. There was an intensity which carried the Chester men with him.'

Alfred Mond was no stranger when he took his seat as one of 377 Liberals in the new Parliament under what was regarded as a brilliant government team including Lloyd George as President of the Board of Trade. More to the point, Brunner Mond & Company was now the most powerfully represented business in the land with three of its directors sitting on the government benches – Sir John Brunner, his eldest son Jack, who was the new MP for Leigh in Lancashire, and Alfred Mond, representing Chester.

Only in one aspect did Alfred Mond lack self-confidence, his speech inadequacies, and day after day, in his study in Lowndes Square he struggled with elocution lessons. He never did overcome a stuttering presentation and, eventually, this was to earn him the House of Commons' epithet 'What, What'. The Times unfairly opined that his bad voice and delivery was impressive only to the caricaturist.

Poker with pipe-smoking Beau Mond at Cambridge.

Young Lloyd George and Violet Mond.

Alfred Mond electioneering in Chester.

Ethel Brunner. A portrait by Solomon J. Solomon, exhibited at the Royal Academy c1901. Solomon's works later included King George V and Queen Mary.

Roscoe Brunner.

Belmont Hall, the home of Roscoe and Ethel Brunner.

25

Chapter 4

THREE years into his political career and Alfred Mond was making great strides at Westminster, not least due to his friendship with Lloyd George, his golfing partner and fellow guest at the country house jollies of the great and good. Mond was a rising political star even though he frequently antagonised the Liberal Party's old guard with his admiration for German methods and his fierce criticism of what he disparagingly termed 'the most popular of British systems, known as muddling through.' A fellow MP, exasperated with his references to European ideals, rebuked him: 'I am not concerned with what occurs abroad. I am an Englishman and, rightly or wrongly, I believe that England is the first country in the world, and I am quite content to go on the old lines my forefathers went on before. What was good enough for them is good enough for me.' Some saw Mond as 'seer of visions, a weaver of dreams', others a 'bloated Plutocrat right down to his fat cigar'. Either way, he was not a politician, or a businessman, to ignore.

Immersed in politics, as he undoubtedly was, Mond still kept a watchful eye on his brilliant father's many industrial struts, the most important of which was the Brunner Mond chemical company whose management had very much passed into the controlling hands of Sir John and Roscoe Brunner. Alfred Mond certainly felt some resentment and matters came to a head in 1909 with the death of his father, the fearsome German chemist who had conquered all to establish the business. Alfred made great play of thanking Sir John Brunner for 'taking the management of 'our' business out of my father's hands' in his latter years, but what he really wanted was a stronger voice for the Mond family in the future running of the company, a surrogate role on the board for his cousin, Emile Mond, who would then be able to keep him minutely informed of what was going on. Sir John was not kindly disposed to the idea but, with a raft of additional shares in his pocket from his father's estate, Alfred Mond was not to be ignored and for the first time in almost forty years of co-operation the fault lines of discord were beginning to appear in the relationship of the Brunner and Mond families.

Alfred Mond also had other matters on his mind, national politics, and many commentators were predicting he was about to be offered a Ministerial post in a reshuffled Liberal cabinet. The Prime Minister, Herbert Asquith, disagreed. To him, Mond was a 'foreigner' to be labelled alongside Benjamin Disraeli and the Prince Consort, 'from over the Channel', to be viewed with patronising pity. Condescendingly Asquith told him: 'The Ministerial jobs have been promised and you are too big a man for an under-secretaryship'. It was a severe disappointment to Mond and he consoled himself that one day he would, himself, become Prime Mininster, or his friend Lloyd George would.

*****

Across Europe in the land of Mond's forefathers, Germany was ominously expanding its naval fleet and the new Chancellor of the Exchequer, Lloyd George, was tasked with implementing a massive counter-balance. Dreadnought battleships were to be the Admiralty's response and he proposed to finance their building through a series of sweeping new taxes. The Conservative Party fiercely opposed the proposal and when the Budget reforms reached the House of Lords they were rejected amidst cries of 'constitutional crisis'. Lloyd George was furious and Mond joined in the attack, although some MPs had reason to wonder at the hypocrisy of the man, for if anyone might have been perceived as a member of the privileged class it was he. Unmoved by the sniping Mond publicly denounced the House of Lords as a 'High Tory committee operating at a snail's pace'. Many years later, and similar to so many MPs with nowhere else to go, he was himself happy to embrace their Lordships.

In order to force through his tax reforms Lloyd George established what came to be known as the 'Budget League', a sort of powerful unofficial financial arm of the Whip's office, and this created considerable friction within the Liberal Party. One forthright MP, Jack Pease, accused Lloyd George of garnering support by dishing out honours and he named Alfred Mond as the largest contributor to the 'Budget League'. Soon afterwards Mond was selected to stand for the safe Liberal seat of Swansea and a Baronetcy was waiting in the wings.

Mond's opponent in Swansea was an indefatigable trade unionist, Ben Tillet, who roared defiance: 'The only reason this Mond is asked to represent you is because this Mond has plenty of money.' Mond's methods, he said, were sordid, wicked, calumnious and dirty, and the best course of action would be to throw him into the docks. Responding more subtly by threatening to put his opponent in the stocks, or on a charge of libel, Mond prevailed without resorting at that time to either extreme, although, presumably to hit back at his detractors, he did try to buy the business of a local newspaper, the South Wales Voice. Stamping into the office of the owner/editor, Ebenezer Rees, Mond placed his cheque book on the desk and said: 'Rees, name your figure. I want your paper and works, lock stock and barrel. I want to ensure that I get back into the House. Your paper will be my platform.' Old Rees was unmoved. 'I'm not selling, Mond,' he retorted, and in doing so gained for himself the reputation of being one of the few men in Wales ever to say 'No' to Mond's money.

Unlike his close-run victory in Chester, a recount was not required and Alfred Mond comfortably swept back to the House of Commons and, in a further leg up the greasy pole of politics, he was raised to a Right Honourable Member of the Privy Council, 'Baronet of Hartford Hill in Great Budworth in the county of Chester'. It was probably an honour due to his support for the Liberals' war chest rather than political performance during the few years in which he had been a Member of Parliament.

Nationally, the Liberals did no more than hold their ground and as the continuing conflict between the House of Commons and the Lords escalated, Mond's former mentor, Sir John Brunner, headed a list of two hunded and fifty prospective Liberal Peers who were to be elevated to force through Lloyd George's controversial Budget. In Sir John's opinion it was a dubious honour – 'Verily the House of Lords is a snobbish institution' – but his family advised him to accept, particularly Ethel Brunner who could see prestigious new rungs on the social ladder if she was to be the daughter-in-law of a Peer. Fortunately for Sir John the crisis passed and he was not called upon to take a seat in the Upper House as Lord Everton.

Sir Alfred Mond

There is no finer sight in creation than the member for Swansea, standing in a full House with a beaming smile on his face, while he instructs Mr Bonar Law on the multiplication table and the geography of Canada. Somebody once said that it was intellect talking through the nose – a description too accurate to be quite kind. Not that Sir Alfred Mond would object, for it is one of his virtues that he is entirely indifferent to petty personal insults. Knowledge, he would say, need not be pretty; it is power, especially when you get a patent before talking about it, and power without prettiness is the essential quality of Sir Alfred Mond's statesmanship. He is ready, like John Wesley, to take the whole world for his parish, or, as he would more humbly express it, his market. If he were at Downing Street, there would brood over all the Empire a thoroughly up-to-date benevolence. Sir Alfred Mond would be the Universal Secretary of State, with Consols at a premium. And if Germany became restive he would say, blandly, 'I know Germany better than the right hon. and hon. gentlemen opposite'. (Loud ironical cheers).

The British Periodical, Truth.

Chapter 5

THE boy from Northwich, Alfred Mond, was beginning to emerge as a leading political figure of his time. A rather stiff, forbidding personality of great stature and wealth, he had acquired a magnificent country house, Melchet Court (formerly Woodfalls), set within one thousand acres of parkland adjoining the New Forest, and, as his biographer notes, he was 'comfortably settled into Englishness'. Additional to politics he was also busy restructuring some of his late father's companies and, as leader of a consortium of Liberal businessmen, he was dabbling in the Press following purchase of the Westminster Gazette, a London circulation daily newspaper.

Mond did not court controversy but throughout his life controversy seemed drawn towards him, like a nail to a magnet, and in the lead-up to war in 1914 he was castigated for his pacifism. The European situation grieved him more than most because his business rationale saw no winners from the crushing financial burden of armaments and, therefore, he was vehemently opposed to war. Unwisely he chose to air his views in a German magazine and this didn't go down well in Britain, especially when 'his' Westminster Gazette followed up with a demand for Britain, not only to keep out of the crisis, but also protect the 'Germans within our gates', i.e. all German nationals, even those suspected of espionage. Fanaticism immediately erupted over him and when his second forename was discovered to be 'Moritz' the

Daily Mail claimed British workmen did not want 'Sir Alfred Moritz Mond, a German Jew', as an ally. It was absurd because at this time Mond was a devout Christian and his children were raised as Christians. However this made little difference to his detractors and a friend of power and influence implored him to leave the political arena, to retire to the country and wait for the war to end. He angrily retorted: 'You can all go to hell – I won't go into the country. I shall go into the government instead.'

There were protests against him everywhere, but unperturbed he went about his business, turning Melchet Court into a convalescent hospital, his London home into a haven for Belgian refugees and his son, Henry, at the age of sixteen, went off to fight in France, one of the youngest officers in the South Wales Borderers. Sir Alfred Mond could hardly have been more patriotic, but to the public at large, whipped up by the mainstream Press, he was not to be trusted and the charges continued to mount. Letters of hatred, letters of accusation flooded through his door and as early as the first winter of the war he was forced to join with Sir John Brunner in a legal action against a Leicester paper merchant who accused them both of being German swines revelling in Belgium and France's 'devastation and misery'.

*****

Mond rode the storm and on went the war. The troops were not home for Christmas and misery piled upon anguish as the politicians at Westminster fought out their own differences. Herbert Asquith's coalition government teetered on the brink of disaster and Mond, as founder of a Liberal 'ginger group' tasked with bringing Lloyd George to power, argued fervently that his friend and political ally was the only man who could lead Britain from the abyss. Lloyd George was chosen and when he rose in the House of Commons he thundered: 'Diplomacy be damned, let us have results'.

It was a defining moment and Mond was singled out to join the new administration as First Commissioner of Works, the highest office that even Lloyd George dared confer upon his old friend and financial supporter, for of all the monstrously rich men he courted at this time, Mond, with his German connections, his name and his ancestry, was the one he probably least welcomed. The enormity of the task facing the government, and its demand for men of a unique business calibre, certainly favoured Mond, but his appointment may also have been reward for past loyalties. Admitting later that there was nearly a Conservative revolt when he put him in the government, Lloyd George remarked: 'No better business brain has ever been placed at the disposal of the State in high office than that of Sir Alfred Mond.'

Fellow travellers and political allies: Mond and Lloyd George.

By now puerile xenophobia was rife in every corner of the land and never did it surface more than in the aftermath of a terrifying night in January 1917 when an explosion of unbelievable magnitude devastated Brunner Mond's massive TNT purifying works at Silvertown in the heart of London's dockland. The blast, said to have been heard as far away as the coast of Sussex, killed seventy-three people, injured four-hundred and damaged over 70,000 properties, including adjoining warehouses, factories, an oil depot and a gasworks. Molten metal showered over London causing many fires with the worst devastation in the nearby, heavily-populated North Woolwich Road and Canning Town. The Stratford Express reported: 'The whole heavens were lit in awful splendour. A fiery glow seemed to have come over the dark and miserable January evening and objects which a few minutes before had been blotted out in the intense darkness were silhouetted against the sky.'

On the following morning speculation was rife that the Hun was literally on the doorstep, that the works was a 'nest of German agents'. A government inquiry was immediately ordered and agents were dispatched to make discreet enquiries in the East End to determine whether there was any evidence to support the popular theory that the explosion was due to enemy, or pro-German activity. Fanaticism against Germans was at its most virulent, the 'hidden hand', the secret influences, the spies who were said to have honeycombed the country and Parliament, and one London magazine openly demanded the government publish a list of 'all men of German stock, or of Hebrew stock who have received distinctions, honours, titles, appointments, contracts or sinecures, both inside, or outside, the House of Commons, Lords and Privy Council'.

In regard to the Silvertown explosion, the East Enders were unable to produce the slightest shred of evidence but to a man they believed German spies were responsible and they named Sir Alfred Mond as directly responsible, because he was of 'German ancestry' as well as a major shareholder in Brunner Mond and a government minister. The official inquiry thought otherwise. It had all been a terrible accident caused by fire in the factory's melt room.

The vilification was unfounded but this was more than could be said of Mond's role in an earlier controversy that also called into question his credibility and patriotism. The allegation centred on the reconstruction of his late father's Mond Nickel Company. As company chairman Sir Alfred Mond stood accused of, in the first days of the war, sanctioning the distribution of three-hundred preference shares to his cousin in Hamburg, as well as other German citizens living in Dresden, Frankfurt, Hamburg, Bonn, Leipzig and Berlin. If true this was a flagrant breach of a King's Proclamation, 'Trading with the Enemy', and an almighty row erupted. The combined shareholding amounted to only 17,775 shares, about one per cent of the total ownership of the company, but it was the principle of the action, not the quantity that was important, and Mond's detractors patiently waited to strike as the Great War drew to a conclusion. They demanded his resignation, or his dismissal from the government, and when neither was forthcoming they claimed it was because of his vast financial support for Lloyd George. The 'New Witness', a weekly publication outside the mainstream Press, rounded viciously on him with a scathing attack by its editor, the author, G.K.Chesterton. The object of the attack, stated Chesterton, was to make the public aware of political corruption and government by the wealthy, 'plutocrats of the ilk of Sir Alfred Mond'. Chesterton claimed Mond was a traitor to be arraigned before a British jury and thrown into gaol over his dealings in the Mond Nickel Company shares.

Eventually the President of the Board of Trade got him off the hook in what the Financial News declared 'a revelation of political trickery', MPs looking after one of their own. It was left to Chesterton and a resolute London barrister, Percival F. Smith, to take up the challenge to try and expose Mond whom, they claimed, had used his wealth and political power to deceive the public. Subsequently the matter went before the civil courts when the Silver Badge Party, a London-based amalgam of frustrated ex-officers and men of HM

Forces, began displaying inflammatory notices in London, claiming: 'Sir Alfred Mond is a traitor; he allotted shares to Huns during the war'. A photograph appeared in the Daily Graphic showing a large crowd gathered around one poster displayed at the Silver Badge Party's headquarters in Charing Cross, and Mond immediately slapped a High Court injunction on the culprits. The offending poster was removed but it was soon replaced with a reproduction page from the Daily Graphic, plus a copy of Mond's writ. The word 'traitor' had been underlined and next to it was added: 'He now squirms'. Later a further notice stated: 'Mond first of all tried to get the police to take this notice down. His next move was to bring pressure to bear upon the landlord to turn us out, but we hope we have frustrated this move. It is now up to Mond to take action in the courts. Has he the courage to do it?'

Mond rose to the bait by placing the matter before a special jury of the High Court Chancery Division, headed by the redoubtable Mr Justice Darling, a former MP for Deptford, and what followed was three days of pure theatre, or perhaps 'pure farce' would be a better analogy, between self-representing defendants and Mond's army of powerful counsel led by his former war cabinet colleague, the venomous Ulsterman, Sir Edward Carson K.C..

In the civil courts British justice is a lie. The only truth is money and whatever we are supposed to believe about each man's innate right to defend himself, barrack-room lawyering is abhorrent to the judiciary, especially at the exalted level of the High Courts. Reports of the proceedings make it plain Percival Smith and the Silver Badge Party were treated throughout with patronising contempt by 'Hanging Judge' Darling who allowed enough proverbial rope to hang themselves. The case hinged simply upon their ability to demonstrate positively that Mond was a traitor, therefore validating the words on the offending poster. However, the principle at stake was whether two eccentric individuals, Harry McLeod Fraser and Henry Hamilton Beamish, on behalf of the Silver Badge Party, should be allowed to bring to task a Minister of the Crown and set a dangerous precedent for every lunatic who ever held a grudge against a member of the government.

Mond's counsel argued that the posters were false and maliciously published; moreover he was not aware of the Mond Nickel Company's share allocation to the Germans during the period October 26 - December 8, 1914, an amazing admission for a chairman such as he who ran his companies with the zeal of a dictator. It was true in the general workings of his business and political affairs he would often become impatient over trivial detail, but on the other hand he was a trained barrister and the intricate detail, the small print, would seldom miss his personal scrutiny, particularly when there might have followed ramifications of a legal nature. It was also impossible for anyone acquainted with Mond to genuinely believe that he did not know what was going on over the Mond Nickel share dealings as, after all, some of the shares were being allotted to his own relatives in Germany.

Under cross-examination by Sir Edward Carson, Fraser said he was the honorary secretary of the Silver Badge Party and he considered Mond to be a traitor in that he had offended against a trust. He was a Member of Parliament and had broken the provisions of the Trading with Enemy Act. Beamish, a newspaper publisher was next to the witness stand. He said that he had been described as a conspirator, but it was untrue. His own father had been an admiral, a one-time A.D.C. to Queen Victoria and he personally had served in the Boer War, India and Ceylon. Prior to the proceedings he had never seen Mond, but he knew him to be an international Jewish financier who was out to destroy Great Britain. Beamish maintained he was not anti-Semite, but he was an anti-corruptionist.

Mond's case was supported by one of his closest political allies, Lord Moulton, the Minister of Munitions, who testified as to his 'loyal and patriotic character', notably in the way in which he had immediately placed Brunner Mond on an all-out war footing in 1915. In fact the company did, indeed, provide around eighty per cent of Britain's explosives but by the time of the bloodiest battles Mond had relinquished his directorship in favour of government office and the gratitude of the nation was more rightly due to Roscoe Brunner and his lieutenants.

Mond's old antagonist Percival F. Smith spoke for Fraser. He maintained that Mond Nickel Company records showed Mond had attended board meetings when the enemy share allotments were made to the German citizens and organisations. Mond countered that he knew nothing of the share dealings and it was not his duty to see that the share register was properly kept. Besides, there were 4,200 shareholders in the company of which only thirteen were considered enemies. He also insisted that, depending upon circumstances, any man who had knowingly traded with the enemy during wartime would have been guilty of committing a 'disgraceful scandal' and would have deserved to have been taken out and shot!

Mond won the day and Judge Darling awarded substantial damages of £5,000.

Meanwhile there was another score to settle in Cardiff, against the South Wales Post accused of having published libellous speeches during the 1918 'Khaki Election'. One speech against him had been made by an alderman of the borough who claimed Mond was a 'foreign agent' and, 'We Welshman have not the adaptability of men like Sir Alfred Mond. We cannot take our nationality on and off like a coat.'

Another was: 'At the Peace Conference and in the diplomacy which follows the war, we do not want any dual loyalty.'

Within the context of fierce electioneering both statements were rather innocuous and it seemed perfectly reasonable for the newspaper to claim 'fair comment' on matters of public interest. Sir Edward Carson disagreed. The words implied Mond was a hypocrite and that he was using his influence on behalf of Germany. This was a foul lie and he had come to be one of the strongest advocates in government for imposing strict terms on defeated Germany.

In the witness box during a five-hour grilling Mond produced his birth certificate to show he was a British citizen and he denied what he termed 'terrible accusations' in which it was claimed he had been sent to the House of Commons as a German agent.

The newspaper withdrew, unreservedly, and formally apologised for the allegations. Damages were awarded to Mond.

That was the end of the legal actions. Mond's name had been cleared although the stigma never fully left him in the eyes of his opponents and many fresh allegations surfaced, but none could ever be substantiated. The arguments in the London trial had specifically centred upon the Mond Nickel Company's allotment of shares to the enemy and Mond's critics whispered that his skin had only been saved by Lloyd George's behind-the-scenes intervention, since his own wife was a registered shareholder of the Mond Nickel Company. In Wales, the South Wales Post's problem was trying to vindicate charges when the opportunities for Mond had simply melted away.

Chapter 6

WITH the war over Sir Alfred Mond was in charge of many of the arrangements for the Peace celebrations and as First Commissioner of Works he oversaw several major public works' projects, including completion of the British War Museum and the building of Sir Edwin Lutyens' Cenotaph, in Whitehall. However, day-to-day, mundane matters were beginning to exasperate him and he told Lloyd George he wished to return to industry. His fiercest critics argued he wanted to leave politics due to Germany's crushing defeat and the floundering of his own political ambitions, whilst others thought it an astute manoeuvre to cajole Lloyd George into granting him high ministerial office. Was there another reason – a return to Brunner Mond & Company following the death of Sir John Brunner?

Whatever, the Prime Minister succumbed. He owed Mond a great deal and by way of inducement offered him the next big office that came into his hands, that of Minister of Health. And so Sir Alfred Mond became one of the Liberal government's 'Big Three' alongside Lloyd George and Asquith, and several commentators were sure he was a Chancellor of the Exchequer in waiting. Describing him at this time as a 'rather flamboyant specimen of a certain class of very rich men', the magazine Everyman commented: 'Sir Alfred Mond would pass unnoticed if he were simply a great landlord seeking a garter, or a mere man of wealth after a barony. But he is more than that. He is a very pushful and skilful hand at the political game. He is immensely rich, acute, cynical, and probably knows quite well what he wants...'.

Mond had only been a year at his new post when, in November 1922, Lloyd George called a General Election. The Liberals were routed as the Conservatives swept to power with the Socialists in formidable Opposition and, although he managed to hold on to Swansea, he was out of place as a backbencher. He continued his unrelenting criticism of Socialism and this made him, and by association Brunner Mond & Company, the butt of many savage attacks by Labour who wanted to remove the capitalist from industry, men, they said, like Sir Alfred Mond. To this end the Socialists failed, but they did eventually succeed in removing him from Swansea when a second snap election was called in December 1923. Mond went down by just 115 votes, sufficient to turn his political career to dust in the coalfields of South Wales. It was a severe shock and, although he staggered to a later by-election victory in Carmarthen, his political star had waned and like a champion boxer he was climbing into the ring for one fight too many. Carmarthen was an agricultural seat and, despite all his bluster, 'Veils for the Veltch', the Welsh farming folk were just as suspicious of his motives as had been the electors of Chester twenty years earlier. Nothing was left to chance and two-hundred Liberal cars ferried voters to the polls to ensure victory and his return to Westminster from where he pledged to expel the Socialists. The more earthy problems of the Carmarthen farmers were soon forgotten.

Occupying the backbenches was bad enough, but then Mond began to fall out with Lloyd George, first over Free Trade and then Agriculture, the latter a subject neither of them fully understood. Lloyd George effectively wanted to nationalise the agricultural industry, to bring it into State control and this stood for everything Mond despised, what he described as a 'blundering attempt at bureaucratic Socialism'. The newspapers said Mond was an ambitious man engaged in a conflict with Lloyd George, a personal conflict because he aspired to fill the Liberal leader's position himself. Finally, he wrote to Herbert Asquith with his resignation from the Liberal Party, declaring that the land policy was a divisive embarrassment. Lloyd George was at his home in Chertsey when suddenly, without warning, normal programmes on the wireless were interrupted to announce Mond's resignation. Lloyd George remarked that 'like another notorious member of his race Mond has gone to his own place'. The rift never healed and Mond knew in his heart he could go no further in politics.

His last stab at politics saw him join the Conservatives but he had been elected by the Liberals in Carmarthen and members of the local association declared him arrogant and contemptuous and wanted nothing further to do with him. The Western Daily Press commented irritably that it would be easier for a camel to pass through the eye of a needle than for a wealthy individual like Mond to swallow the land programme: 'No more convincing compliment could, therefore, be paid to its importance than that it should have driven Sir Alfred Mond to find a new spiritual home in the Tory Party'.

When Mond took his seat on the Conservative benches in the House of Commons there were howls of protest and Lloyd George wondered what thirty pieces of silver might buy. Few men, of course, hold office of state without possessing an enormous ego and Mond was no exception as he tried to persuade the Conservative Prime Minister to appoint him Chancellor of the Exchequer, a post he still craved. Not surprisingly Stanley Baldwin turned him down and with nowhere else to go in politics his return to industry was inevitable.

Sir Alfred Mond's home, Melchet Court in Hampshire.

Symbolic of a passing age: The unveiling of John Brunner (above) and Ludwig Mond's statues at Winnington. Old Mond gazing out for all eternity, as his son would have said, 'viewing the future from the plateau of history'.

*Devastation at Silvertown Works.
Right: The Silvertown Memorial.*

*The 11th hour, the 11th month...
The Armistice celebrations in 1918.*

*Sir Alfred Mond as Minister of
Works commissioned The
Cenotaph in Whitehall.*

44

Top left: A crowd gathers in Charing Cross to read the Silver Badge Party poster accusing Mond of being a traitor.

Top right: The Big Three: Lloyd George, Mond and Asquith.

Middle: Sir Alfred Mond, Minister of Health, with Queen Mary.

Left: Brunner Mond war memorial unveiling by Sir Alfred Mond at Winnington.

45

Chapter 7

FOR a brief interlude the sufferings of the Great War gave way to a world at peace and the troops were home to share in the success of Brunner Mond & Company to whom the chairman's baton had passed from father to son. It was a seamless transition and as the undisputed, patriarchal head of an international business, Roscoe Brunner was keen to embrace a new dawn and new challenges. A pillar of the community, a justice of the peace and a deputy lord lieutenant of Cheshire, he served on this body or that organisation, chaired one committee or another, and to most everyone who ever came into contact with him he was as an affable English gentleman, without airs and graces, devoted to his workforce, his father's company and the town of Northwich. The local newspaper wrote of him:

> He possesses an immensely sanguine temperament and always takes an optimistic view of affairs. His deep voice and his resounding laugh reveal a zest and a joy for life; he is carefree, cheerful, detached from the disagreeable and the ambitious; he has an adored and beautiful wife...

Roscoe's wife, Ethel, remained something of an enigma. Her acts of charity in the district were legendary, but then with so much wealth and opportunity she was able to indulge in whatever she pleased. There were those who looked upon her as a woman of marked social and artistic gifts, an accomplished singer, a sculptor and a collector of fine arts, but others would point to her impulsiveness and volatile moods that could quickly swing from the sublimely generous to the absurdly malevolent. In one instance she would richly reward a servant and, in another, truculently dismiss the entire household staff, a situation that often prevailed upon Roscoe Brunner's alacrity to restore dignity and calm. Her explosions of anger were familiar to her husband who was often the butt of her sometimes uncontrollable raging. One story is told of how, in a fit of temper, she ordered the chauffeur to set fire to Roscoe's expensive new car, simply because he had not consulted her before purchasing it. When the chauffeur refused to carry out her orders she dismissed him. Below stairs there were whispers that Roscoe Brunner may have found solace elsewhere, but if he did then the intimate details certainly never reached the ears of his wife. Ethel Brunner said of marriage: 'From closest observation, the one conclusion I've been led to is that the one sphere in which a woman cannot possibly live her own life is that of marriage. She has to obliterate herself entirely.'

She was nobody's fool, but she was strong-willed and, occasionally, so obnoxiously forward that some thought her a 'bitch without scruples', determined to do whatever she pleased, and anyone who stood in her path was destined to be unceremoniously shouldered aside. In the fullness of time she would meet her match in Sir Alfred Mond.

All who knew the Brunners, dependent of course upon their own relationship, had a differing view of Ethel and it is only as an author that she positively reveals anything of her inner self. Between 1917 and 1924 she penned three novels, her first a slim volume of 150 pages 'Celia and Her Friends', and then followed a short 'comedy play' 'The Elopement – Celia Intervenes', and in 1919 'Celia Once

Again' in which the heroine embarks on a Continental tour and describes the people she meets. Her final work, and apparently her best, although one critic dismissed it as 'devoid of hardly any storyline', was 'Celia's Fantastic Voyage' in which she discusses at great length a variety of more or less important topics relating to social reform and the analysis of industrial and political motive.

In the context of her death these provide a fascinating insight into her own character as the heroine 'Celia' seems, undoubtedly, to have been fashioned from Ethel herself, her alter ego, the person she desired to be. Celia, she wrote, was obsessed with the idea that she would be able to manoeuvre things into happening, that she never did a single thing in the whole of her life without a motive. This was Ethel Brunner to a tee and the final hours of her life would resonate to the following passages:

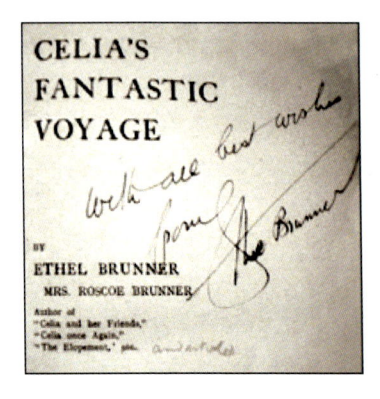

Signed frontispiece Celia's Fantastic Voyage.

> 'Whether it was to order a new hat, cross a room, sit down in a chair, or take a cup of tea with an uninteresting woman, Celia always had a motive. She said herself that she never made a friend or shook hands with a person except with a view to using them for something. She lived an altogether very involved and intricate life, densely surrounded by motives…'

> 'You who can do anything with anybody, with your charm and brilliance. I didn't think there was a person living you could not manage…'

Several of Ethel's major characters were obviously sculpted from the Brunner and Mond families, including 'Stalybrass' who was surely her father-in-law's old partner, Ludwig Mond. She portrays Stalybrass as an over honest, over earnest, uncompromising figure who dismissed, or demolished, matters that should not have been dismissed. He was '...the strident and really unreasonable Labor (sic) Leader whose truculent, trestle-legs planted so obstinately on what he constantly and loudly referred to as free soil.' Then there was a former 'Government Minister' overshadowed by the powerful industrialist, Lord Tyneforth. The ex-Minister was almost certainly Sir Alfred Mond, whilst Lord Tyneforth was Sir John Brunner whom Ethel greatly admired in all but one matter, i.e. his refusal to accept a peerage. Through Lord Tyneforth, Ethel narrates the rise of a great industrial concern at Millington Hall, in the county of Dampshire, in other words Brunner Mond & Company at Winnington Hall, in the county of Cheshire. A reference to the 'Letchmeres' comes from Lord Delamere who advocated the public flogging of John Brunner and Ludwig Mond for having the temerity to build a chemical aberration on the banks of the River Weaver. Lord Tyneforth:

> I well remember the late Autumn of 1878. That was a year for me. It was a rare cold, clammy, dreary and depressing season, that one when I signed the papers purchasing the estate of Millington in the County of Dampshire to build our works on, with Millington Old Hall and Millington New Hall included. For there were two great old mansions there, an old one and a new, bang up, one against the other. The one old and low and rambling, Elizabethan black and white, the other enormous and stately in stone... It was do or die, sink or swim – and there's plenty of water here for both purposes. It was for the water – and other things of course – we bought it, but principally

for the water. Water for the process and water for the freight. On that day in the Autumn of '78 we were perished with cold and frightened well nigh out of our senses at what we were going to do. The solicitors for the Letchmeres did not seem very impressed by me. They didn't like the deal. Knew what it was for, and very naturally didn't fancy the poor old spot being desecrated by chimneys, coke ovens and blast furnaces and what they knew we meant to do besides. The disappointment, the heartaches, the bad debts, the loads we carried with us day in day out. Our place nearly closed time after time. Every single Saturday that we paid our men for years was a day of crisis for us.

Roscoe Brunner is plainly 'Sir Timothy Strutt' and a definite clue is discernible here. Ethel describes Sir Timothy as 'an admirable pendant to his wife' and he had about him 'an enormous expectation of recognition of himself and his wants or ideas from people'. As to Celia, i.e. Ethel, she was a 'dainty and delightful hostess', fortunate to possess an exceptionally large circle of witty and amusing friends. A charming lady, she had a great deal of money, through no fault of her own. In fact she was able to spend as much as she liked without bothering her head as to whether she could afford it or not. 'But she is not selfish and her great idea is that some day, sometime, she'll be able to do something large and productive towards helping the world along and that the money will come in very useful when she finds her opening'. In her latter years Ethel discovered an outlet for her philanthropic desires as she immersed herself in fund-raising to help find a cure for tuberculosis.

Celia's devoted admirer was always Peter Blenerhasset who was something of a mystery. The heroine was said to be undecided about him and in an autobiographical sense he remains a mystery since all of Ethel's major characters appear to have had a place in reality.

Could she have been having an affair behind Roscoe's back, or was she merely using Peter as a male vehicle to indulge her own vanity? If she did have an extra-marital suitor (the only reference in family documents is to a London solicitor by the name of 'Pierre') then she was far too circumspect to allow the matter to become public and to their circle of friends she always appeared the perfect wife.

Had she lived Ethel Brunner may have widened her horizons and the scope of her talent, but, on the other hand, she was neither driven by need nor ideals and her work smacks of the same self-indulgence that so marked her life. All her novels were rather quixotic and short on substance, but reasonably popular because she was an outstanding self-publicist and seldom missed an opportunity to push herself, in newspapers, magazines and on the new-fangled wireless. The name 'Ethel Brunner' was well known and in the days following her death, black-ribboned portraits of her were displayed in the windows of several of London's leading bookshops. There has since been a modern upsurge in reprint sales, one current reviewer describing the content of two of her novels as 'seriously peculiar with

> WITH HIS PERMISSION,
>
> I DEDICATE THIS LITTLE COMEDY
>
> ## TO MY HUSBAND,
>
> WHO FOR OVER EIGHTEEN YEARS HAS BEEN
>
> A HUSBAND-PAL TO ME.

Ethel Brunner's dedication to Roscoe.

pages of turgidity and eccentricity'. More charitably, her publisher of the time glowingly noted: 'Mrs Brunner writes brilliant dialogue, and is gifted with penetrating insight into modern minds and manners. Her characterisation, although keen, is kind for she is too clever to be cynical.'

Ethel Brunner, the Lady Bountiful from the lofty heights of Belmont Hall, basked in this new-found fame as she was called upon to open even more bazaars and garden parties, distribute school prizes, lecture on housewifery and serve on committees of numerous charities. She also played a leading role in local politics by organising extravagant fund-raising fetes, soirees, masked balls and dinners. Like Sir Alfred Mond she despised the march of Socialism, 'the New Order' as she put it, 'the Extremist party with comic opera economics'. To her, Conservatism was the only means of its defeat.

It's fair to say she was not well liked within the Brunner and Mond families and only her father-in-law, Sir John Brunner, had seen fit to humour her impetuousness if only for the sake of his grandchildren. How poor Roscoe viewed his wife's enthusiasm for the Conservative cause, and what embarrassment he must have encountered, is not documented, but years later he too switched parties, although any notion of him entering politics was invariably dismissed with a scornful laugh. Not for him the complications and futilities of a political career – he did not have a second to spare beyond his family, his business and Cheshire.

Ethel Brunner in her early years as an author.

Chapter 8

FROM the moment he succeeded his ailing father as company chairman, Roscoe Brunner adopted a most unconventional approach to business management. Rather than the boardroom at Winnington, the centre of his modus operandi was Belmont Hall where, with his trusted lieutenants James Herbert Gold and John Gibb Nicholson, he formed an unofficial management triumvirate to ensure Brunner Mond's fortunes went from strength to strength.

Almost needless to say, Ethel Brunner went out of her way to encourage these gatherings for although women were fervently demanding their rights they had hardly begun to knock on the door of male-dominated bastions of industry. It suited her down to the ground that the Brunner Mond boardroom was manoeuvred to Belmont Hall and, tennis and croquet over, she would join the triumvirate to learn more of the company's business dealings than all the rest of the directors put together. She was certainly encouraged to voice her opinion and her furthest thought was to undermine her husband's and, therefore, her own position.

In 1923 the company marked its Golden Jubilee with a glittering dinner during which the town clerk of Northwich, Mr J.A. Cowley, praised Roscoe Brunner, the new man at the helm, a 'worthy son of a worthy sire' who, he said, had attained the chairmanship by sheer merit:

> We who depend so much upon Brunner Mond and Company for our wellbeing consider that the destinies of this great company are in safe hands. There is a noble band of workers, and young and energetic though they may be, they need a gentleman to lead them, and in Mr Roscoe Brunner the great administrators of this firm can have no better leader.

One who did not share Cowley's 'safe hands' optimism was Sir Alfred Mond who was widely recognised as one of British industry's most incisive minds. Shipbuilding, coal, cotton and heavy engineering may have been in the grip of recession but he was far more optimistic for the prospects of the chemical industry and, besides, Brunner Mond had just recorded a record annual profit of over £1 million. Yet it wasn't enough for Mond and, in a self-fulfilling prophecy, he said he wanted an even greater business of international reputation, more powerful throughout the markets of the Empire, throughout the markets of the world.

Privately, Mond disapproved of Roscoe Brunner's triumvirate style of management but, still engrossed in the shenanigans of Westminster, he was not yet ready to fully commit himself. The signs were there, however, that he intended to take over, to influence and control the entire British chemical industry and, sooner or later, he was going to be a dangerous bedfellow for Roscoe Brunner.

And so it was to prove when Mond found himself dumped in the political wilderness, defeated at Swansea, his only House of Commons' seat the Strangers' Gallery. He consoled himself by setting off for India to holiday with his old friend Lord Reading, the Viceroy. He knew his political career had run its course and his stab at Conservatism had reaped little recognition. Industry, on the other hand would allow him to impose his own brand of radicalism, unfettered by the electorate. His closest associates always felt he was destined to be an industrial statesman, provided, they reasoned, his fellow directors were prepared to be ruled by an 'immensely rich, acute and cynical autocrat'. And here was the rub when, prior to leaving for India, he rejoined the Brunner Mond board after an absence of ten years. A man who had aspired to be Britain's Prime Minister was never going to be content with a subservient downtable directorship.

The chemical industry, he argued, was ripe for a vigorous new approach, 'rationalisation', a term he is generally accredited as being the first to use and whose very mention still furrows the brow of workers the world over. His thinking, crystal clear, was summed up in a memorial publication following his death in 1930:

> Freed from office, industry and the immense schemes of industrial reorganisation that had already shaped themselves in his mind, instantly claimed him; and his severance from his former political association meant little more to him than the dropping of an investment that had lost its efficacy and the seizure of one that still seemed sound and serviceable. The project he was meditating went beyond all party lines.

His biographer later went further: 'He ruled his industrial enterprises with the courage and vision of a dictator. He was utterly ruthless in forcing his issues through. He rejected sentimentality in pursuit of his purpose and had to reconcile himself to the idea of making enemies.'

Fortuitously for Mond, his return from India coincided with the most serious acrimony to date in a legal bear-pit in which Brunner Mond had been scrapping for years with Lever Brothers, the world's leading makers of soap. The autocratic head of Levers was Sir

William Hesketh Lever who had long vied with Sir John Brunner for the distinction of being the Liberal Party's chief benefactor, but these were mere skirmishes of what was to follow. Roscoe Brunner managed most business dealings on behalf of Brunner Mond, except when the enemy was Hesketh Lever and then Sir John Brunner had personally taken up the cudgel, although rather than sound business rationale he was driven by an intense dislike of his rival whom he considered a despot. The two men were constantly at one another's throats over contracts and complicated agreements because, essentially, Brunner Mond held almost a monopoly on the supply of alkali, an indispensable raw material in the production of soap. Hesketh Lever was convinced he had been duped out of £1 million by Brunner Mond and in the First World War the conflict plummeted into such personal venom that the two protagonists became as entrenched as the battle lines on the Somme. One judge, offering a silent prayer, hoped he would never again see either company, a sentiment echoed by Sir Alfred Mond who wrote to Roscoe Brunner declaring the troubles 'typically British, petty, shortsighted and certainly not likely to benefit either party'.

By 1924 Sir John had gone to his grave but Hesketh Lever was spitting fire, accusing Brunner Mond of reneging on a contract through which his company was supposed to have received alkali at a cheaper rate than its competitors. Lever wrote to one of his colleagues: 'Without mentioning names, except that I do not include the present or past chairman of the company in this remark, there is an entirely changed atmosphere towards the contract... I feel very uneasy and uncomfortable because I am satisfied we are not today getting a square deal as we were entitled to under the contract.'

Roscoe Brunner indignantly denied the allegation and, as it could not be proved, there the matter might have rested. Then, totally out of the blue, Brunner dispatched an amazingly frank letter admitting there had, after all, been a flagrant breach of contract and, even more deplorably, Brunner Mond had drawn up bogus invoices to cover the scam. An astonishing, foolhardy revelation, this was bound to lead to litigation, although no-one at the time, or since, has ever been able to explain why Roscoe Brunner confessed, whether he was a recklessly naïve honest broker, or covering up for someone else. Decades later I.C.I.'s official historian, W.J.Reader, thought Brunner simply lost his nerve, but what he failed to appreciate was that, by no stretch of the imagination, was Brunner a chairman to act alone.

His confession letter, dated March 1, 1924, coincided precisely with Sir Alfred Mond's return from India, his firm planting of feet under Brunner Mond's boardroom table, and, as the company's most powerful shareholder, he was the most obvious colleague for Brunner to consult. If this was so, and it seems extremely likely given the circumstances, then Brunner was swimming in dangerous waters. Politicians are adept at playing both ends against the middle and a heavyweight like Mond knew every trick in the book. So when, a week later, the confession letter was read to the Brunner Mond board it whipped up a furore from which Roscoe Brunner would never recover.

Mond had lived up to his reputation of 'possessing the knack of chopping off the head of an opponent with an undisturbed air of smiling benevolence'. Absolute power was his for the taking.

The Brunner Mond board of directors before Sir Alfred Mond's return.

John Gibb Nicholson (left), James Herbert Gold (centre) and William Hesketh Lever.

The centre of Brunner Mond's empire in 1910.

59

Chapter 9

A SINGLE topic above all others provoked fierce argument at Belmont Hall and it centred on Roscoe Brunner's refusal to consider a permanent move to Brunner Mond's head office in London. To his wife, London was the rightful place for the head of an international business that had long since outgrown its parochial roots. She had busied and buried herself in a 'provincial little town' for over twenty years and Northwich was hardly a centre of the literary and publishing world. She yearned for the bright lights of London society where 'vulgar' capitalists were breaking down the established values of position and title.

Brunner would have none of it. It was anathema to him. His life was based on regularity and routine, simple and fulfilling, and his friends and his public service were in Cheshire and, besides, whenever he needed to be in London, there was always a company apartment at his disposal in Cavendish Square. In one of her 'Celia' novels, Ethel Brunner obliquely raises the very question of London and there is no doubt she was relating Roscoe's view when she penned the opinion of 'Sir Timothy Strutt':

'I find this business life in London doesn't bring out too successfully the good we have in us, if by chance there is any. City life feeds the passions and starves the emotions till they very nearly perish away, and the passions get overgrown and big. If it's not one, it's another. Pride, envy, emulation, oh – everything, whilst one's true feelings can't make themselves felt.'

Celia (Ethel) had a different view: 'It's an excellent place, if you would give some consideration to your way of life in it. My life is my own, why isn't yours yours?'

Whatever the merits, or otherwise, of London, Roscoe and Ethel Brunner were in agreement it was the place to find a husband for their daughter, Shelagh who, at twenty-six and hardly a great beauty, was approaching spinsterhood in the whirlwind, self-indulgent world of the 1920s. A debutante, like her mother before her, Shelagh had enjoyed the finest education and finishing money could buy and, with her father's wealth behind her, she was not short of suitors. None matched the expectations of Ethel who was fearful that, left to her own devices, her 'horsey' daughter was more likely to walk to the altar in a riding habit.

As mothers do, Ethel's anxiety increased when, in 1924, Shelagh was a bridesmaid to Roscoe's niece, Joyce Morgan Brunner, who married William Worsley, the eldest son of Sir William Worsley, Bart. of Hovingham Hall, Malton. It was a grand occasion conducted by the Archbishop of York and prominent reports in the London society pages served only to rouse Ethel's resolve to find Shelagh a fitting husband, of the highest social standing. She may also have cast an envious glance at Sir Alfred Mond's family since, in terms of connections, his children mixed freely with some of the rich and fashionable socialites of the day, sponsored as they were by their father's political standing and, to some extent, his German ancestry. One of Mond's daughters, Eva had already married the son of Lord Reading, the Viceroy of India, and in their turn, her sisters, Mary and Nora, were close friends of Edwina Ashley and 'Dickie' Battenberg, and many others from the families of the Cassels, Hirschts, Wernhers and Teks, some of whom were cousins to the royal family. Others in this circle of Mond family acquaintances included Freda Dudley Ward, the close friend of the Prince of Wales.

Ethel Brunner was not a woman to be upstaged by anyone and mere common suitors were far from her sights. If necessary she was prepared to trawl all of Europe to find a knight errant on a milk-white steed to claim the dowry and fair hand of Shelagh. What followed perfectly demonstrates her ability to spin the wheels of manipulation, the quixotic novelist skilful at advancing her own story. And what a story Shelagh Brunner's marriage turned out to be.

First there was a famous clairvoyant who informed mother and daughter that a whirlwind romance would follow with a nobleman from Central Europe: 'The match will be an immediate love-at-first-sight. Your husband will be a handsome, cultured, wealthy young personage, and, in some subtle, mysterious way, horses are connected with your betrothal.' Straight from the pages of a modern Jilly Cooper epic, the Brunner family then, allegedly, attended an American-style rodeo at Wembley and here, before Shelagh's smitten eyes, appeared a dashing and daring young horseman who, later in the evening, and 'quite by chance', happened to be seated at the next table during dinner. Rising from his fellow guests, 'Mayfair ladies and gentlemen' we are told, he walked over to Shelagh, bowed and offered his hand.

He was twenty-three-year-old Prince Ferdinand Andreas de Liechtenstein, nephew of the Crown Prince of the tiny Alpine principality of Liechtenstein, a dot state on the map of only sixty-two square miles. For title, prestige and immense connections the Prince was considered one of Europe's most eligible bachelors. His father was a personal friend of King George V; his aunt, Princess Marriza, the accepted leader of Viennese society and his great uncle, Count Andrassy, was a former Prime Minister of Hungary. Betrothal followed and Shelagh was swept off her feet when the dashing Prince sped across Europe to obtain sanction and the passing of a special Bill in the Liechtenstein Parliament, enabling him to claim his bride as the first member of the Liechtenstein Royal Family to marry a commoner. It was a fairytale script, but the reality was quite different. The entire introduction had been set up through the gentry's famed marriage arranger, Viscountess Massereene and Ferrard, of Lancaster Gate, and the Prince, though well known in European diplomatic and financial circles, was considered by many to be a penniless, long-on-pedigree philanderer. Later, his brother, Johann, also married into money, a cattle baron's daughter from the Prairies of Texas whom the American newspapers dubbed the 'Panhandle Princess'.

Engagement: Shelagh and the Prince.

Still Shelagh's marriage to a handsome prince was the catch of all catches and Ethel Brunner was determined to spectacularly land this one. She had always harboured a tendency to be outrageously ostentatious, it was part of her make-up, and now she could turn her self-perceived sophistication and exquisite taste into creating an extravaganza, the society

> **BRIDE FOR A PRINCE.**
> **ROMANCE OF MISS SHELAGH BRUNNER.**
>
> Prince Ferdinand Andreas de Liechtenstein, second son of Prince Edouard de Liechtenstein, is to marry Miss Shelagh Brunner, only daughter of Mr. and Mrs. Roscoe Brunner, of Belmont Hall, North-wich, Cheshire.
> Prince Ferdinand, who is 23, was born at Salzburg, Austria. The home of his family, which is a branch of the Catholic Liechtenstein line, is Schloss Rosegg, Carinthia.
> Miss Brunner is the granddaughter of the late Sir J. T. Brunner, Bt. and her father is chairman of Brunner, Mond, and Co., Ltd. Her mother, who was formerly Miss Ethel Houston, is the author of "Cecila's Fantastic Voyage," "Celia Once Again," and other books.

63

wedding of the year. She threw dinner party upon dinner party to extol the merits of her daughter's pending marriage to Prince Ferdinand. It was the greatest social coup she could have engineered and as the wedding guest list soared to over seven-hundred, many booked into suites of stately rooms at London's major hotels, it became more akin to a list from Who's Who?. There were to be Princes, Princesses, Counts and Countesses, Barons and Viscounts and scores of legations from the countries of Europe. Not for Ethel was this to be a parochial, or even a county wedding and, as it was necessary for Shelagh to adopt the Liechtenstein Royal Family's Catholicism, the splendour of London's Brompton Oratory was chosen in keeping with some of the most fashionable weddings of the day.

The great ceremony in St Wilfrid's Chapel took place on Wednesday January 14th, 1925, and Ethel went far beyond the extreme to turn it into a fantasy wedding with which to publicly impress London society. It was to be Shelagh's wedding, but Ethel's crowning glory. They would certainly talk about this one, and so they did. Parts of London were brought to a standstill and at the conclusion of the spectacle, 'just too unique for anything my dear!', there were calls for future 'marital exuberance' to be restrained in the capital.

For a wedding outside of the British royal family the media interest was unprecedented. Long before the big day Ethel was feeding details to the newspapers and society magazines, not just that a British commoner would be saying 'I will' to a Corinthian prince, but that this was going to be a ceremony of gold, an 18-carat event of unsurpassed magnitude. By high-noon thousands were gathered outside Brompton Oratory, a truly amazing scene afterwards reported across the globe. One Canadian newspaper commented: 'Tecs from Scotland Yard tried to push back the swarming flood of eager curiosity-seekers. In vain! Crushed in the press, the Prince and the

Princess-to-be could scarcely reach the altar. The mob proceeded to throw the place into further pandemonium by wedging into niches reserved for saints' statues which tottered on their pedestals.'

The 'Lady Correspondent' from Northwich also enjoyed an unforgettable occasion:

> When the bride and her father entered practically the whole of the great church was monopolised. In their eagerness to catch a glimpse of the bride in her golden gown and golden coronet, women stood on the seats, and men too, scrambled for a view, one resourceful woman having supplied herself with a periscope. Suburban visitors, uninvited to the ceremony, rubbed shoulders with such society celebrities as the Dowager Marchioness of Bute, Princess Yourievsky, Lady Ponsoby, etc etc. When about to kneel with the Prince at the altar, the bride discovered that one of her bridesmaids, Miss Iris Ford, was not in her place, and at once delayed for a few moments. The verger, who had closed the door to prevent the hundreds who desired to pack themselves into the already full church, was informed and a policeman on guard told that only the bridesmaid was to be admitted. Immediately Miss Ford made an appearance.

The bridesmaids, eight in all, including Miss Iris Ford and the Princess Gabrielle of Liechtenstein, were attired in gowns of gold lace, embroidered with rubies, all topped with head-dresses in gold tissue. The best man, Count Terence Erdody, was in spectacular Hungarian nobleman's uniform of the 15th century, rich purple, velvet and silver, and the scene was described as one of 'unsurpassing splendour'; the great white marble pilasters and shining gilded cornices of the sanctuary adding to a magnificent collage of colour, complemented by the mass choirs and music of the Brompton Oratory.

On Roscoe Brunner's arm came the bride, apparently 'unbelievably stunning', in a robe of gold lace, her long full train lined with gold tissue, a head-dress topped with a gold coronet, and even her prayer book was in gold, embossed with the Prince's initials and crown. At the conclusion of the marriage rite the bride and bridegroom knelt whilst the priest read aloud a personal telegram from the Pope: 'The Holy Father imparts his Apostolic Benediction to his dear children, Ferdinand de Liechtenstein and Shelagh Brunner, on their marriage.' Afterwards, the guests retired to Claridges for a formal reception, the 'Lady Correspondent' remarking that it was on a 'scale of sumptuousness rather easier to imagine than describe'. The wedding party took over a suite of three state rooms bedecked in gold and with the famous Claridges' orchestra playing amidst the palms and flowering shrubs it was altogether a brilliant scene, '...the happy bridegroom with his radiant bride, the throng of distinguished guests in their charming frocks, gleaming jewels and magnificent furs'.

Interviewed by the Press, the Prince, fluent in English, German, French and Italian, spoke lovingly of his wife. She was a fine horsewoman and tennis player and he would be introducing her to his own speciality, that of mountaineering. He hoped too that she would soon learn to speak German, the language most commonly used by Liechtenstein's population of just 10,000. It was intended, he said, that he would be given management responsibility for some of the vast estates owned by his uncle, Crown Prince Johann II.

How Ethel Brunner savoured the moment, the limelight, the exalted position in society she had always craved. It was, as was her way, over the top and it brought its nemesis, for hardly had the euphoria of Shelagh's wedding subsided when the storm clouds began to gather for a shattering climax.

BIG WEDDING IN LONDON

Prince Ferdinand of Leichtenstein and Miss Brunner

London, January 14.—One of the most brilliant weddings of the New Year was celebrated today at Brompton Oratory, when Prince Ferdinand of Leichtenstein was married to Miss Shelagh Roscoe Brunner, of Norwich, England, in the presence of several hundred guests, including many society notables.

The bride wore gold lace with a gold veil over a dress of gold material and carried a gold prayer book. Eight bridesmaids wore mediaeval dresses of gold material and carried bouquets tied with gold ribbons. Count Ferenaz Erdody, as best man, wore the costume of a Hungarian lord of the Middle Ages. A big reception was held later at one of the principal hotels.

The happy couple.

Brompton Oratory.

67

Bridesmaids and best man, Count Erdody, done up to the nines. The wedding was described as 'one of the most theatrical, fancy dress affairs of the season', Prince Ferdinand, apparently, the only member in the ceremony 'not got up in carnival attire'.

Left: Desert honeymoon.

Below: The wedding makes international headlines.

THE WINNIPEG EVENING TRIBUNE, SATURDAY, MARCH 7, 1925

Movement in London for Fewer and Quieter Weddings After Adventures of Golden Bride

Stunning Miss Shelagh Brunner, the Cheshire Beauty, Weds Prince Fedidard Andreas de Liechtenstein, a Young Austrian Nobleman With Great Eclat.

DAUGHTER OF FAMOUS HOUSE

Chapter 10

AT the conclusion of the wedding celebrations Roscoe Brunner returned to his desk in the sure knowledge that, in spite of the Lever trouble, his fellow directors were right behind him and, as a matter of course, he was re-elected company chairman. He was also tasked with heading a special board committee to deal with the Lever writ, although by final settlement a year later he had been ousted with the tacit acquiescence of the same colleagues, kicked into the long grass in favour of Sir Alfred Mond. The public reason was ill-health and it's true he was struck down by a debilitating attack of shingles, an illness that wracks at the nervous system and often brings temporary lapses of memory and acute depression. Shingles hit Roscoe Brunner hard and for several months, during the summer of 1925, he was treated with morphine as he convalesced away from the rigours of business management and the political machinations that had descended on the boardroom of Mond, his 'temporary' stand-in.

August and September was the holiday period and Ethel Brunner was busy putting the finishing touches to a Belmont Hall garden party of gargantuan proportions. She had wowed London with her daughter's wedding and now it was the turn of Cheshire and the Warrington Conservative Association to sample her extravagance at an occasion she ensured would be 'Royal' in magnitude and magnificence. No less than fifty coaches and hundreds of cars ferried the guests from Warrington to Belmont Hall and over 1,500 supporters, including lords and ladies, mingled in the manicured grounds to enjoy a lavish tea and entertainment of prodigious proportions. The local newspaper summed it up as a 'splendid occasion with rousing speeches and glorious weather'. Roscoe Brunner was conspicuous by his absence, but the association secretary took the opportunity to heap praise on him for his support, particularly his 'telling platform contribution' on the eve of the 1924 general election in Warrington. There were few, remarked the secretary, who could speak with greater authority than Mr Roscoe Brunner who was, justifiably, regarded as one of the most important industrialists in England.

Compliments also showered on Ethel Brunner who held court as never before, a 'charming hostess who throughout the day moved about chatting genially with her guests, making all feel thoroughly at home'. In response to the formal speeches she said she was a writer, wife of an enormously successful businessman, and she had before her a large programme, writing articles and propaganda in opposition to all forms of Socialism whose doctrine was nonsense. She thanked guests on behalf of her husband and cheers welcomed her pronouncement that he was expected to return to his former self within a few weeks. And return to his old self he did. In September 1925, he accompanied hundreds of Brunner Mond workers on their annual outing to Blackpool and, amidst prolonged applause, declared that he was 'absolutely recovered – very fit, indeed'.

Meanwhile, in the Brunner Mond boardroom, the Lever affair rumbled on and in the end it cost the company £1 million in damages, a colossal sum, equivalent to almost £50 million at 2016 monetary values. The board capitulated on the advice of Sir Alfred Mond's personal expert counsel, probably those whom he had entrusted to fight his post-war libel actions. The first payments to Levers were orders drawn on the Old Bank of Northwich, on November 1, 1925, one for £277,000, the other for £262,500. A third order followed on November 30, for £194,000. The balance lay with the High Court.

It has since been said that Brunner Mond's behaviour in the Lever fraud 'struck at the roots of commercial morality' and, anxious to preserve the company's reputation, the board ordered an internal investigation. A formal report was prepared and the contents were clearly controversial as, to formally close the matter, members of the board insisted upon personally witnessing the document being locked away in the company safe. A sealed copy was also dispatched to the company solicitors, with the explicit instruction it was never to be opened without a formal resolution of the board. To this day, there is no record of the document in the otherwise extensive Brunner Mond/I.C.I. archives.

A few incidental documents do survive from the Lever debacle, including a letter, dated December 1925, dispatched by Sir Jack Brunner to his brother, Roscoe. Addressed from the National Liberal Club, London, this informs 'Ross' that 'Jack and Alfred (Mond)' had attended a meeting with Francis D'Arcy Cooper, the chairman of Lever Brothers, to arrange what the two companies intended to tell their shareholders. Sir Jack explained: 'He (D'Arcy Cooper) is going to show nothing in his balance sheet referring to the action and to say nothing at his shareholders' meeting except that their lawsuits were satisfactorily settled.'

Creative accountancy, or cooking the books, but it seems the Brunner Mond board was prepared to pursue the same course at its own annual meeting, although this did not quite happen. Perhaps Sir Alfred Mond's hand was forced because, without mentioning fraud, he gushingly admitted that a £1 million payment had been made to 'our friends Messrs Lever Brothers' to settle a business matter. The decision, he said, had been a 'wise one' and, buoyed by announcement of a generous share dividend, most shareholders swallowed it, although a few must surely have wondered how the company could possibly have afforded £1 million.

What went on privately is not known – the board's secrecy and subterfuge saw to that – but, publicly, Roscoe Brunner's name was never linked to the affair until after his death. Indeed, as High Court documents reveal, Levers themselves absolved the Brunner Mond board from 'knowingly, or intentionally deceiving, or defrauding' and, above all, this included the then chairman, Roscoe Brunner. Furthermore, in the month following payment of the last instalment of the £1 million, Brunner was selected by his fellow directors to serve on the board's finance and policy committee. Would they have done so if they thought he had been responsible for the fraud?

The real villain was, undoubtedly, James Herbert Gold, the third member of Brunner's triumvirate. A lawyer, company secretary and the youngest director, Gold, who may have been related to the Brunner family, was of a nature that delighted in audacity and he would certainly have enjoyed putting one over on Levers. At closure of the affair he was forced to resign, although the board, paranoid over potential damage to the company's standing, paid him handsomely to keep his mouth shut. He received a lump sum of £5,000 (£0.25 million in today's money) and an annual pension of £3,000 (£160,000), a hell of a price to pay if, as company historians would have it, Roscoe Brunner was to blame for the Lever fraud. Gold went on to invest heavily in a business involved with automatic photography but he remained, for ever, persona non grata and, conspicuously, his name was absent from a list of surviving former directors invited, forty-five years later, to attend Brunner Mond's centenary dinner.

Chapter 11

1926

Queen Elizabeth II is born. The flying ace Alan Cobham completes a mammoth 16,000-mile return flight from London to Cape Town; Grand Prix motor racing launches at Brooklands; The world land speed record is shattered on the south coast of Wales; The fledgling BBC is earmarked to become a public corporation. An average house costs £619, a packet of twenty cigarettes one shilling (5p), a pint of milk threepence (1.5p). 'Imperial' is the buzzword – an Imperial Conference establishes the Commonwealth; Imperial Airways offers passenger flights from London to India; Imperial Chemical Industries (I.C.I.) is forged, a commercial behemoth of the 20th century, the pride of Britain, a bellwether for the nation's economy.

State of Emergency: The General Strike, the greatest strike in British history, commences on May 3, 1926 and lasts for nine dramatic days. Two million workers down tools; Armoured cars patrol Oxford Street; The Flying Scotsman is derailed; Tin-hatted volunteers drive the newspaper lorries, trains and buses; Peeresses man canteens in Hyde Park. The nation is in turmoil.

THE sonorous chimes of Big Ben mark the passing of an old year and for the aristocracy and wealthier classes optimism is in the air. Britain seems on the verge of recovery after the Great War and life has never been better. In these first heady hours of 1926 the bright young things party to the Charleston in Mayfair, at Claridge's and the Park Lane Hotel, bob-haired flappers in short skirts, young beaux in their Oxford bags, all excitedly embracing the Roaring Twenties of opportunity, the era of the Jazz Age, the silver screen heartthrob Rudolph Valentino and Scott Fitzgerald's Great Gatsby.

Two-hundred miles away the little parish church of Great Budworth heralds the occasion in its own more sedate way and, at nearby Belmont Hall, members of the Brunner family gather to toast a new chapter. Their paternal head, Roscoe Brunner, had been marooned for months in the commercial wilderness, but fully recovered from illness and the Lever fall-out he is ready to resume his position at the head of Brunner Mond's chemical empire, and by way of celebration he is eagerly anticipating moving to a new home he and his wife had purchased Hartford Lodge, close to Northwich town centre.

For all concerned this was going to be a vintage year of opportunity. But of course, it wasn't – it was an illusion. In 1926 Britain was to become a nation of uncertainty, political turmoil, social distress and industrial strife, and a nightmare awaited Roscoe and Ethel Brunner. They would not live to hear the bells of Great Budworth Church, or Big Ben, to welcome 1927.

Meanwhile the national coal industry had been in turmoil for years and the divisions were wider than ever at the start of 1926 as the pit owners and miners locked horns over wages and working hours. Neither was prepared to give an inch and many eminent politicians, none more so than Sir Alfred Mond, voiced their opinions on the best way to achieve a lasting peace. Mond regularly monopolised The Times' letters column to expound on his theories and to cite Germany as a shining beacon of hope. It wasn't his most diplomatic argument and the miners responded by angrily raking over the embers of his German ancestry and his patriotism.

Closer to home Mond had a pressing personal business problem – what to do about Roscoe Brunner who, in name at least, remained chairman of Brunner Mond. Officially Mond had been keeping the seat warm, a first lieutenant to steer the ship during the captain's absence, but this wasn't Mond's way. His political career may have been in tatters but, possessed of an enormous belief in his own abilities, he had grasped power with both hands and, if he had refused to live in Lloyd George's shadow, he definitely wasn't going to defer to Roscoe Brunner. The future of the entire British chemical industry, as Mond saw it, rested on himself and he had no intention of allowing it to remain in the control of those he contemptuously dismissed as a 'preponderance of exceedingly puzzle-headed men waiting until things happen, the complete neglect to endeavour to foresee possible difficulties'.

By the early months of 1926 Roscoe Brunner was regularly attending board meetings as he eased his way back into day-to-day management. Then, quite suddenly, he placed his resignation 'in the hands of the board' and we can only guess as to whether he was pushed, he jumped, or he was seeking a vote of confidence in the wake of the Lever affair, a 'Me or Mond' assurance? If it was the latter he was on a loser, because his boardroom colleagues were overwhelmingly in thrall to Mond and his grand ideas and, on March 4, 1926, Roscoe Brunner's proud leadership came to an abrupt end. He was, of course, succeeded by Mond who, six weeks earlier, had penned a resignation letter of his own, severing twenty-five years with the Liberal Party.

To Ethel Brunner, Mond's appointment was the worst imaginable kick in the social teeth. No longer would the Lady Bountiful be able to pick up the Belmont Hall telephone and introduce herself as 'Mrs Roscoe Brunner, the wife of the chairman of Brunner Mond'. She was livid and the Belmont Hall servants soon began to sense an intensely strained atmosphere as their mistress remorselessly pressed the master to confront his accusers and, if necessary, seek shareholder support to challenge Mond's takeover. Harold Dorrington, the butler-valet, remarked: 'She was considerably worried over her husband being forced to give up the chairmanship of Brunner Mond & Company. She thought the other partner (Sir Alfred Mond) was not treating Mr Brunner fairly'. Another servant went further: 'I think Mr Brunner was out of his depth with Mond. Mrs Brunner hated Mond's guts'.

Ethel Brunner had always deeply mistrusted Mond – he was a little too obsequious, too clever by half – and, though she was not averse to fighting dirty, she knew a successful challenge rested entirely on Roscoe. A good old-fashioned British stiff upper-lip he stood his ground and refused, even if it was a fight he might have won as he was still widely perceived amongst thousands of smaller shareholders and workers to be the company figurehead, the rightful heir to Sir John Brunner. For all his family connections Sir Alfred Mond was viewed as an outsider, a controversial, confrontational politician.

Politics has never been a place for the thin-skinned and Mond, with characteristic, intimidating self-assuredness, held the upper hand. There was no hope for Roscoe Brunner. Friendship could only mean so much and, besides, Mond was already conjuring up a radical 'oil-from-coal' scheme to join Brunner Mond in a worldwide consortium with America's Chemical & Dye Corporation and Germany's IG Farben. The plan involved setting up a £25 million holding company and Mond, the weaver of dreams across the floor of the House of Commons, made Roscoe Brunner an offer which, under the circumstances, he could hardly refuse: Accept a new career challenge, or drift into semi-retirement. Unfortunately Brunner wasn't chiselled from granite like Ebenezer Rees, the editor/owner of the South Wales Voice, and the upshot was he soon came round to saying 'Yes' to Mond's invitation of a leading role within a proposed 'oil from coal' holding company to be set up in London.

So late in his career, and given his long-held resistance to uprooting from his beloved Cheshire, Brunner had reservations, but these were countered by his wife who was sold on the idea and absolutely delighted. London was the place she had always wanted to be and, now, a pseudo duchess, mother-in-law to a European prince, she saw herself enthroned in a grand mansion where she would be able to entertain the indolent socialites of the metropolis. In the euphoria she forgot the warning her father-in-law, Sir John Brunner, had so often impressed on Roscoe. Never trust Mond.

*****

The protagonists in the national coal crisis had been lurching towards all-out war for months and the eruption came when the miners walked out demanding 'Not a penny off the pay, not a minute on the day'. On May 1st, 1926, the owners closed the pits and, two days later, Britain was in the grip of a General Strike as over two million workers downed tools to bring the wheels of industry to a shuddering halt. The response was nationwide, but, more than anywhere, the T.U.C. was determined to paralyse London, to force the government to intervene on the side of the mineworkers. Instead, fearing anarchy, the Prime Minister, Stanley Baldwin, ordered the army to set up barracks in the capital and patrol the streets with tanks and armoured cars to maintain law and order and guarantee delivery of essential food supplies. At first it was ugly stalemate as the dockers, printers, power station workers, railwaymen and transport workers brought the capital to a virtual standstill. Revolution was in the air and Winston Churchill, the Chancellor of the Exchequer, took personal charge of publishing a daily news-sheet, the 'British Gazette', to rally the government cause, whilst the strikers countered with their own version, the 'British Worker'.

Then the tide began to turn when an estimated 300,000 middle and upper class volunteers who disapproved of the strike, 'holding a pistol to the nation's head', rallied to the government cause. Young men in Eton ties acted as railway porters, Oxbridge graduates, city gents and retired army officers manned the power stations, drove the delivery vans, the buses, trams and trains. It had suddenly become a class struggle and as Ethel Brunner, en route to Roehampton and Green Cottage, struggled through the unprecedented chaos she would gladly have joined the titled ladies, dames and debutants who were manning the 'scab' canteens in Hyde Park. She would most certainly have approved of the Roehampton polo players who, mounted on their ponies, pitched in as special constables, armed with cut-down polo sticks for truncheons.

The government refused all overtures to parley and after nine days and against overwhelming odds, the T.U.C. capitulated. On May 12, the General Strike was called off and the mineworkers were left to fight their own battle, which they did, resolutely staying out for six months before returning to work longer hours on less pay.

It was during these tumultuous days that Ethel Brunner settled in at Green Cottage, to commence her search for a palatial mansion and also to assist Princess Shelagh in the final throes of pregnancy. She was already familiar with the Roehampton and Putney district as she had personally leased Green Cottage for the newly-wed 'Royals' on their return from honeymoon, initially as a temporary arrangement although the princely philanderer, Ferdinand, had found it a most convenient base for his participation in the London social scene of wild parties and loose morals.

Princess Shelagh was days away from giving birth and nothing but the best would suffice for Ethel Brunner, Prince Ferdinand's mother-in-law from hell. None other than the Court physician was engaged, Lord Dawson of Penn, who a few weeks earlier had delivered our current Queen Elizabeth into the world. On Saturday May 8, 1926, on the sixth day of the General Strike, a son, Christopher, was born at Green Cottage to Princess Shelagh and Prince Ferdinand.

Back in Cheshire, the shareholders of Brunner Mond were gathering for the company's annual meeting presided over with much posturing by the recently anointed chairman, Sir Alfred Mond. He found it impossible, he said, to refuse the board's request for him to succeed Roscoe Brunner who had been feeling the strain of responsibility for some time. He wished him well and hoped he would soon be restored to his normal health and activity. It was a whitewash, but, luckily for Mond, one substantial shareholder, Ethel Brunner, was not present to put the record straight about her husband's health and recovery.

For the time being Ethel's priorities were elsewhere. She had found her dream home, virtually on the doorstep of Green Cottage. It was Roehampton Court, on the Mount Clare Estate, near to Richmond Park, a handsome Georgian mansion with a fleeting similarity to Belmont Hall, but far more imposing. With its sweeping carriage drive and forty rooms Roehampton Court (now the Maryfield Convent) was described by the auctioneers as having 'dignified proportions, tasteful fittings and a feeling of rest and harmony'.

Ethel was ecstatic and quickly persuaded Roscoe to acquire the property. Some records show he purchased Roehampton Court for £20,000, £1 million in today's money, others that he leased the place. The latter seems more likely. Either way, Ethel attacked the project with her customary alacrity and penchant for pretentiousness as she personally commenced directing an extravagant programme of refurbishment. She had her hands full. Shelagh and the Prince had sailed for the Continent on an extended holiday and she was running Green Cottage, caring for the welfare of her new grandson, and penning her next novel, as well as attending to the beautification of Roehampton Court. Meanwhile Roscoe Brunner, in temporary residence at the company's Cavendish Square apartment, was finally beginning to sever the umbilical cord of Cheshire and was finding London life infinitely more pleasant than he had envisaged. Mornings he would spend at the Brunner Mond offices, afternoons at the Bath Club, his gentleman's club in Dover Street and, for the first time in a quarter of a century of high-powered industrial management he was able to take in Wimbledon, the rowing at Henley and test match cricket at the Oval. He was also regularly attending Brunner Mond board meetings which, for the most part, were now being held in London. Occasionally he would weekend with his wife at Green Cottage, to monitor progress at Roehampton Court and, also, discuss their fund-raising efforts for Dr Spahlinger's tuberculosis research in Geneva.

THE CATCH OF THE SEASON.

From Punch, February 1926: Sir Alfred Mond and Stanley Baldwin. The date is significant. A few weeks later Roscoe Brunner resigned as chairman of Brunner Mond to leave the way clear for Mond's 'takeover'.

1926: A cauldron of civil strife and unrest.

*In the midst of the General Strike Ethel Brunner began
her search for a London mansion..*

Roehampton Court, from sales brochure of 1926.

A newspaper cutting showing Green Cottage.

Chapter 12

ROSCOE Brunner had endured the most traumatic year of his life, but relaxing in London it all seemed well behind him as he eagerly anticipated Sir Alfred Mond's return from the United States and confirmation of the 'oil from coal' international agreement. Unfortunately, he was totally unaware a new player had entered onto the scene, Sir Harry McGowan, the chairman and managing director of Nobel Industries Ltd, the British arm of the international explosives industry. For months McGowan had privately promoted a very different proposal involving a total merger of the British chemical industry and, alarmed by the international discussions, he hastened to New York to make one last stab at talking Mond round to the idea of Brunner Mond joining forces with Nobel Industries, United Alkali and British Dyestuffs. McGowan and Mond were made for each other, gunpowder and bank notes, 'the most damnable inventions known to man', according to the 18th century campaigner William Cobbett. McGowan's intervention succeeded and, unceremoniously, Mond tossed his much-vaunted 'oil from coal' deal into a New York trashcan. With it went the London holding company and Roscoe Brunner's hopes.

On October 6th, 1926, Mond and McGowan took their berths aboard RMS Aquitania as she sailed out of New York bound for Southampton. One of the most handsome liners afloat, Aquitania was like a great Georgian mansion, oozing luxury, grandeur and opulence, and with a passenger list tending towards the pages of Burke or Debrett's. By day, Harris tweed, Chanel jerseys, indolent conversation and energetic sport; by night, a sudden increase in tempo, a blaze of jewels, the gleam of ivory shoulders, the formality brilliance with which aristocratic English life was so perfectly at ease. It was here, amidst the grand setting of the Palm Courts, the Palladian lounge and the Louis XIV dining room, that the two captains of industry formulated their Magna Carta, their own Bill of Rights, what came to be known as the 'Aquitania Agreement', from which spawned one of the most far-reaching and profound mergers in British industrial history, the creation of Imperial Chemical Industries. The future for millions of pounds of investment, thousands of workers and entire communities was mapped out on the high seas and, somewhere in the grand scheme, there was bound to be a price to pay, but what Mond and McGowan could never have foreseen was personal tragedy lapping at the bow of RMS Aquitania.

Sketched on four sheets of Cunard Line notepaper, the 'Aquitania Agreement' came to be the template for Sir Alfred Mond and Sir Harry McGowan's masterplan as they set themselves weeks to fashion their new empire. Throughout the six-day voyage they worked night and day, and nor did they rest on the seventh, for within hours of disembarking at Southampton they were putting the final pieces in place to take over the entire British chemical industry, lock, stock and barrel. McGowan, a flamboyant bon viveur of gigantic energy, had risen from an obscure Glaswegian background and, though the two men were poles apart, he brought single-minded determination to Mond's table and once they had set their minds to a merger, there was only the grand scheme of things to consider. McGowan may have conceived the British merger plan, but it was Mond, a major public figure, who would take on the mantle of chairman, although absolute executive authority was to rest with them both. They also agreed on a business name, Imperial Chemical Industries, a choice that did not go down well with the Registrar of Companies, later prompting Mond to complain, 'We are Imperial in aspect and Imperial in name.' Eventually they got their way and, afterwards, Mond went further by announcing that I.C.I.'s markets would be the Empire, 'the largest single economic unit in the world'.

The immediate task was to prepare a convincing case to carry shareholders of the four merging companies, to offset the threat of aggressive commercial competition and Britain's inability to compete for a fair share of the world's markets. It was a compelling argument and in the fullness of time was to prove correct. And so, on Monday October 25, at a special meeting of the Brunner Mond board, Roscoe Brunner learned of his fate. Sir Alfred Mond, one of that breed of powerful men capable of disdainfully obliterating the inconsequential, had totally rearranged the pieces on his chessboard and Brunner had become as dispensable as an election opponent in the valleys of Wales.

However, remarkably, Brunner did not seem in the least put out and, instead, cheerfully set off for Cheshire where he was to chair a meeting at Winnington Works and also attend, as principal guest speaker, a dinner of the Northwich Conservative Association. He was in good heart and if his business career was, indeed, over then no-one would have guessed. A rapturous welcome greeted him at the Conservative dinner and the Northwich Guardian remarked that he was in 'fine form', 'radiantly happy' and that '...no director of the large chemical firm of Brunner Mond is held in greater respect by the workforce who idolize him'.

The newspaper also printed at length Brunner's speech in which he complimented the Conservative government and outlined why he had recently decided to forsake the Liberal Party. Several hundred guests were present, including several of his fellow Brunner Mond directors, and not a hint of anguish was detected, even though the I.C.I. merger was a major topic of conversation. In short, Roscoe Brunner appeared to be good-naturedly accepting the shifting tectonic plates in his business career, although, as the newspaper commented: 'It is a very great disappointment locally that he is not on the new board of Imperial Chemical Industries...'.

Nine days later Roscoe Brunner and his wife were found dead, but there was to be no stopping the runaway I.C.I. express. Mond wrote to the Press:

> The formation of a great combination in Germany and other parts of the Continent, the existence of the great chemical groups has forced the leaders of the chemical industry in this country to the conclusion that the time has arrived for the British and Imperial Chemical industry to endeavour to form equally a united front. It is not intended to destroy the identity of the autonomy of the invided units composing the new company to be formed. The boards of these companies will continue to operate the respective industries with which they are most intimately associated. The board of the new company will form a supervising and connecting link in finance and policy, in exchange of knowledge and information, and will enable the British chemical industry to deal with similar large groups in other countries on terms of equality, enable them to speak with a united voice, and, instead of leaving it to individual units to make arrangements for the world's competitive conditions as best they can, will give them all the authority and prestige and advantages of a great combination...

It transpired that Mond and McGowan never had any intention of allowing the converging companies significant rights to control their own destinies, and almost total abandonment of individual identity was to follow once shareholders had been appeased. Mond insisted: 'We are on trial before the eyes of the entire world, and especially of our fellow citizens and of the Empire. We are not merely a body of people carrying on industry in order to make dividends, we are much more; we are the object of universal envy, admiration and criticism, and the capacity of British industrialists and British commercialists and British technicians will be judged by the entire world from the success we make of this merger.'

RMS Aquitania, Sir Alfred Mond and Sir Harry McGowan (right).

Chapter 13

DISBELIEF and shock swept the worldwide workforce of Brunner Mond & Company when the mind-numbing news of the deaths of Roscoe and Ethel Brunner began to break in the early days of November 1926 and nowhere was the grief more acutely felt than in Cheshire, the cradle of the great chemical undertaking and the home of 'Mr & Mrs Roscoe'. For over fifty years Brunner Mond had dominated the life and fortunes of the district and practically every family, in every street for miles around, had at least one member of the household working at 'The Chemic'. There was no rule that jobs went from father to son, no agreement that generation should follow generation, but the lineage continued, unbroken and unyielding. For so long at their head had been Roscoe Brunner whose life had now been cut short in the most tragic and unimaginable circumstances.

Amongst the many who stopped to mourn and remember was a rising young engineer, Jack McCormack who would never forget the dreadful sorrow of that November morning as the flags were lowered in Northwich: 'At first it was just a rumour, spreading like wildfire from one man to the other, but nobody knew for certain,' he said. 'And then it was confirmed by one of the managers. You cannot imagine the esteem with which Roscoe Brunner was held and his death, in the tragic circumstances outlined to us, was a terrible shock. Whatever had happened during the previous year regarding Mr Roscoe's removal from the chairmanship, he was Brunner Mond and we were all stunned beyond belief. I was a draughtsman with Brunner Mond in the 1920s, originally indentured as an apprentice fitter. I didn't, of course, mix in the exalted circles of the Brunner family, but we all knew Roscoe Brunner as a charming man with a quiet demeanour. He was a prominent figurehead and when he gave up his position as chairman of Brunner Mond we heard that his wife reacted violently, accusing him of cowardice.'

Officially, the workforce was told only what could be contained in a bland four-line statement pinned to communal noticeboards and from that moment, insisted Jack McCormack, the matter was never again formally mentioned. All that remained as a mark of respect on the day of Roscoe and Ethel Brunner's funerals was a short suspension of duties at the company's works and offices across the world. 'That was it,' bitterly recalled Jack McCormack. 'Mr and Mrs Roscoe were wiped off the face of the earth and they were instantly consigned to history by the company hierarchy. Roscoe Brunner's epitaph, for all his efforts and the prosperity he had brought to Brunner Mond, was four miserable lines...'

It was left to the Northwich town clerk to formally sum up the feelings of Northwich and Cheshire. Mr Brunner, a thorough English gentleman, he said, had died a martyr to duty:

> He had the natural English sympathies with all forms of suffering and want, and he was the embodiment of all that was good and uplifting. All who had dealings with him testify to his high character, and Northwich people in particular always entertained a high regard for him. If there was one trait in his character that stood out above all others, it was his kindness of heart. He will be remembered not only as a great employer of labour and a great man

in the world of commerce, but as a kindly Christian gentleman, of the noble life he lived and the good work he accomplished. Sir John Brunner, in the great calamity that has befallen him, will find some measure of comfort and solace in the thought that those who knew him best, since the late Mr Brunner had lived amongst them so long, have a depth of sympathy for him which cannot be expressed in mere words. Mrs Brunner was a woman of great personal charm and undoubted ability, and took a tremendous interest in her husband's welfare and business relations. Those who knew Mrs Brunner best knew her as a kindly lady and one who was prepared to go to any lengths to right a wrong. Her consuming desire to help the consumptive of the country was entirely in keeping with her general character. The council has crossed swords with Mr Brunner as representing his company at times, but of him it can be said with truth that his motive was pure. There was no bitterness – just dogged tenacity of the business mind. We knew him so well that we testify that we have lost a really true friend. We in Northwich will be much poorer by our loss.

The editor of the local newspaper was equally glowing in his praise of Roscoe Brunner, although of Ethel Brunner he was less than fulsome: 'She was possessed of an attractive personality and a winsome disposition. She was an ideal hostess to the guests at Belmont Hall who were many and varied. She was honourable to a degree, and her generosity was well known...'.

These were hardly the words Ethel Brunner would have chosen, but then her strong Conservative views had not always held favour with the editor of a staunch Liberal newspaper. At society level it was a different story: 'Slim and pretty she seemed the embodiment of youth; in fact no-one would have guessed her to be the mother of a grown-up daughter. Her parties, both in London and in the country, were always successful and attracted crowds of interesting people. She dabbled in literature and her last novel, Celia's Fantastic Voyage, created quite a stir when a luncheon party was held in her honour at the Lyceum Club. She was a woman of the most generous impulses, and a great many people have lost in her their most valuable friend.'

The Press, understandably, had a field day in the aftermath of the tragedy and by the following Monday, November 8th, the strident, sensational headlines fuelled the curiosity of a morbid crowd who besieged Wandsworth Baths, a most incongruous setting for such a high profile inquest. Outside, enormous queues stretched back a hundred yards on both sides of the entrance, everybody eager to hear, first-hand, how a wealthy and privileged couple had succumbed to such a deadly fate.

Samuel Ingleby Oddie.

The Westminster coroner, Samuel Ingleby Oddie, immediately put his foot down and ruled that only journalists, 'representing the general public', were to be permitted to witness the proceedings. Ingleby Oddie, unique in his day in that, simultaneously, he covered three separate areas of the city, including Roehampton, was reckoned to be a coroner of the old school, 'benevolent in attitude but punctilious', but he was, also, often controversial. He had once famously remarked: 'The only wise people are bookmakers. The rest are fools.'

In his younger days he was a GP in New Malden and had then pursued a career in law at the Central Criminal Courts, notably as a member of the prosecution team during the trial of Dr Crippen. Keenly interested in the psychology of crime he had been a founder of the

London-based Crimes Club whose members included judges, barristers and crime writers, including Sir Arthur Conan Doyle, author of Sherlock Holmes. Upon his death in 1945 Ingleby Oddie was said to have brought 'clarity and strength of mind' to his inquest proceedings; he believed in ascertaining the facts and he hated subterfuge in any form. Whether he always adhered to this mantra is a matter of opinion.

In the Brunner inquest his basic duty was to determine how, when and where the couple had come to their unexpected deaths and, as was the way in those days, a 'puppet' jury of locals was roped in at short notice, twelve good men and true who could not have failed to have been prejudiced by the voluminous newspaper reports of the tragedy.

The opening witness was Roscoe's brother Sir Jack Brunner (John Fowler Leece Brunner, 2nd Bart.) who was visibly shaken by the appalling events. He stated that Roscoe was fifty-five years of age and had recently given up his house, Belmont Hall, in Cheshire, and had taken Roehampton Court, near to London, but at the time of his death was not occupying either residence. Roscoe was a director of public companies. His brother's wife, to the best of his belief, was forty-nine. He said he had last seen Roscoe on October 25th, at a board meeting of Brunner Mond, held in Cavendish Square. His brother had been chairman of Brunner Mond since 1918, but he had vacated the chair and was succeeded by Sir Alfred Mond.

> Coroner – The vacating of the chair would be I suppose at the request of the board of directors and for good reason?
> Sir John Brunner – Yes, it was stated at the annual meeting of the company that it was on account of his poor health.
> Coroner – And was there any other reason?

Yes – There were serious business troubles.

Coroner – For which he, as chairman, I take it, had to take responsibility?

Yes, he had to take responsibility.

Coroner – Do you know of your own knowledge whether the giving up of the chairmanship was rather felt by him?

Yes, it was a serious blow to him.

Coroner – Can you tell me when the new board of the new company, which I understand is being formed, was constituted?

The board is not yet constituted – it is only proposed.

Coroner – But tentatively has the board been suggested?

Yes.

Coroner – And a new company formed in which there is a combination of Brunner Mond and other companies?

Yes.

Coroner – Was he suggested as a director of this new amalgamated company or not?

No sir. His name was not among those published.

Coroner – Do you know that it would have been a great disappointment to him?

It was a very severe disappointment to him.

Coroner – At what date did he get this information?

On October 25 at the board meeting I have referred to.

Coroner – Has he written to you since upon the subject?

No.

Coroner – You mention his health in your statement. What do you know?

He had been very ill for quite two years.

Coroner – Do you know the nature of his illness?

He had a very serious attack of shingles. A very nervous disease; very painful.

Coroner – You have never heard of him speak of suicide?

No, never.

Coroner – Did you know he had a revolver?

No, I was not aware of it at all.

Coroner – As regards the terms upon which he and his wife lived, were they ordinary domestic terms?

They were very affectionate. From time to time, she was moody and, if I may say so, somewhat difficult.

Coroner – Do you know that she had taken an interest in her husband's business?

She had his interests very deeply at heart.

Coroner – It follows therefore that she would share his disappointment at his not being on the board?

Yes, she felt it very acutely.

Coroner – Do you know from what you heard from him what his attitude was about his wife interfering in his business affairs?

It very greatly distressed him. He had loyally accepted the decision of his colleagues, but she would not accept it and caused him considerable difficulties, which greatly distressed him.

Coroner – Suppose your brother had discovered that his wife had been round to various newspaper offices endeavouring to interest them in his not being on the board, can you tell me what the affect would probably have been upon him?

I believe that if that had come to his knowledge he would have been exasperated beyond measure. I believe, I would

go as far as to say, it would have turned his brain.
Coroner – Do you know of any other trouble which might have supplied an adequate motive for his taking his life?
I know of nothing else.
Coroner – Would the loss of the directorship be more serious to him from the point of view of finance or pride?
It was pride only, not finance.

The next witness was the nursemaid, Ruth Buckle who was in no doubt the Brunners were perfectly happy when she had visited the nursery a few hours before their deaths. She said that she did not hear revolver shots despite the nursery being above and only one room removed from the bedroom in which the bodies were found.

'Between maid', Bella Scott, 15, of Northwich, was the last person to see the Brunners alive and she too confirmed they appeared on 'good terms' on the night of their deaths. The Prince, she said, had left for a holiday and the Princess followed on July 23. Afterwards Mrs Brunner had been in charge of Green Cottage. Mr Brunner had stayed at the house during two weekends prior to the tragedy.
Bella Scott – I opened the door when they came. I made tea and took it up to the writing-room.
Coroner – What were they doing?
They were sitting in front of the fire talking. Mr Brunner asked me to phone over for the chauffeur. That was about 6.50. Mrs Brunner said she would have her supper after Mr Brunner went about 8 o'clock. I reported that in the kitchen.
Coroner – And the next thing?
The hall bell rang. I went to the hall and Mr Brunner was there. He said he wanted the chauffeur. The chauffeur came

round and I went to the writing room. When I got to the writing room they both answered the door, saying, 'Hello, who's there?' Mrs Brunner said, 'Don't come in'.

Coroner – Did you hear any altercation?
No.
Coroner – What did you do then?
I went downstairs and told the chauffeur that I had told Mr Brunner he was there.
Coroner – When did you go up again?
About 9 o'clock. I went up two or three times and knocked at the door, but got no answer and came away.

Mrs Nellie Attwell, housekeeper/cook and wife of the Green Cottage butler, stated that Mr and Mrs Brunner appeared quite friendly towards each other. The witness said she went upstairs because the maid, Bella Scott, could not get an answer.

Coroner – You went up to the room somewhere about 10?
Yes.
Coroner – Were you the first to go in?
Yes.
Coroner – The light was on?
Yes.
Coroner – You thought they might have fallen off to sleep?
Yes. I felt uneasy and went back to the writing-room to have another look.
Coroner – You opened the door?
Yes.
Coroner – When you entered the room you saw Mr and Mrs Brunner on the floor between the foot of the bed and the writing desk?

Yes.

Coroner – You then went downstairs and called the chauffeur?

Yes.

Coroner – When the chauffeur came out of the room he said, 'It's finished'?

Yes.

The chauffeur Thomas Holdstock stated that on the day of the deaths he picked up Mrs Brunner at about 3pm and drove her to the Bath Club. Afterwards they proceeded to the city and he waited for an hour outside the Financial News office in Queen Victoria Street. From there they went to pick up Mr Brunner and drove to Green Cottage.

Coroner – What time did you get back?

About 6 o'clock. I asked Mr Brunner if he was going back to town. He said he would require me at about 8 o'clock. I went to have tea but a telephone message came over to my wife saying that Mr Brunner was ready to go back then. That would be about 7 o'clock. I drove to the cottage and got a maid to announce I was there. I continued to stay in the car. As a rule, you could hear Mrs Brunner talking, but I heard nothing and it was very unusual to wait for Mr Brunner. Mrs Attwell went up to the room but could get no answer. It was now nearly 10 o'clock. Mrs Attwell then called me in an agitated voice. I went up and saw Mr and Mrs Brunner lying at the foot of the bed. I was just going to shake Mr Brunner and tell him it was 10 o'clock when I noticed blood on the floor. I did not touch anything.

PC Thomas Whitwell, the first police officer to arrive at the scene, described how he found the bodies lying at the foot of the bed. Mrs Brunner, he said, was lying on her stomach, her face turned towards the bed and Mr Brunner was lying on his left side across his wife's body. His right arm encircled her waist and in his right hand he was holding a revolver. He was lying face down on Mrs Brunner. Both were fully dressed and Mrs Brunner was wearing a hat and coat. Mrs Brunner had a bullet wound on the right side of the neck, below the ear, Mr Brunner a wound in his right temple.

Coroner – Were there any signs of a struggle?
No sir.
Coroner – Were there any writings bearing on the death?
There were notes all over the room, but not bearing on the death.

Dr Alexander Stowell, of Northwich, stated he had been medical adviser to the Brunners for over fourteen years. He said he had attended Mr Brunner for a very severe attack of shingles on the face and scalp in August or September of 1925 and following this attack, Mr Brunner had suffered from very severe pains that had been relieved by morphine. Dr Stowell said he had seen Mr Brunner from time to time until his death. 'He told me that there were times when he could not remember things, names or faces, and sometimes had to be prompted. I last saw Mr Brunner on October 27th. He was looking very ill and worried and said he was suffering from pains in the head and could not sleep.

Dr Athelstane Nobbs, the Police surgeon, presented a post-mortem report and testified that on his arrival at Green Cottage, at 10.45pm, he was able to ascertain that death had only recently occurred. He said there were untidy papers everywhere, but there was no sign of a struggle, although he thought it curious that a drawer was open above the bodies. Photographs were produced by the police to show the interior of the writing-room. The photographer, Det. Insp. William McBride, noted: 'There is a hat on the floor... a stain on the floor, between the foot of the bed and sideboard.'

In his summing up the coroner said it seemed plain that Brunner had shot his wife and then himself:

'He was a very distinguished businessman, and had for many years been associated with the firm of Brunner Mond and for a time was chairman of this very important company. During his tenure of the chairman's office there was some financial trouble, not as regarded the stability of the firm of course, but some question of contract, or some trouble which resulted in heavy loss. As chairman of the board of directors he would no doubt be held responsible for that loss, and it would appear that it was on account of that unfortunate business transaction that he was requested to vacate the position of chairman of Brunner Mond & Company.

'As you can well understand when that took place he would be very distressed, worried and unhappy. We know from the evidence of his medical adviser that he was so worried that he could not sleep, and that he was highly nervous, that he suffered from a well known nervous affliction, and was mentally confused and by no means normal. On top of this distressing question of the loss of his position as chairman, which was a matter affecting not his pocket as his pride, came the next blow.

'There is apparently some huge combine of important business interests being formed, including Brunner Mond &

Company, and when these large firms amalgamate, positions have to be found on the board for all the directors of the various companies which are amalgamated. When the new board was tentatively formed, or the names put forward, it did not include the name of Mr Roscoe Brunner. That information came to his ears on October 25th.

'There again you can well understand what a blow that would be to his pride, coupled with the distress he must have suffered from losing the chairmanship... He procured the revolver, brought it to London, surely not with any intention of killing his wife, but with the intention of killing himself, and at this time was apparently not aware of the fact that his wife was actively intervening in the matter of his not having been placed on the board of the huge new combine. Can we not properly infer that on the night of the tragedy, the conversation in the writing room at Green Cottage must have been about the worrying absence of Roscoe Brunner's name from the Board of Directors of the new company. In the course of this discussion, is it not extremely likely as almost to amount to a certainty, that she then divulged what she had been doing, as she thought, in her husband's best interests, in the matter of hawking this grievance about the various newspaper offices? If that were so, does not that explain the whole tragedy?

'Cannot you see what happened – a man driven to despair and distraction by losing his position finding his wife interfering in this way? Cannot you understand how, to a man of his temperament and his position that might well have been the last straw which caused his mind to lose its balance entirely? If so, his original intention of killing himself, which may be inferred from the evidence, seems to have been suddenly transformed, in a moment of intense frenzy, exasperation, and irritation, into an insane impulse also to kill his wife. If that is your view you will have no alternative but to return a verdict of murder in the case of Mrs Brunner, and of suicide while of unsound mind in the case of Mr Brunner. He was a frenzied madman, and yielded to an insane impulse, killing not only himself, but his wife.'

And so, without so much as retiring to consider their verdicts, the jurymen, knowing their place in the presence of their 'betters', found exactly according to Ingleby Oddie's directions, 'murder' and 'suicide whilst temporarily insane', the latter standard inquest-speak to ameliorate the then criminality of suicide.

On the day following the inquest, amidst what the newspapers described as 'utmost secrecy', the bodies of Roscoe and Ethel Brunner were cremated at St John's, Woking. Their final journey was almost as bizarre as the closing chapter in their lives. From Wandsworth Mortuary two enclosed cars carried the coffins on a long detour through Kingston, Esher and down the Portsmouth Road, before turning back to Woking and twice circling the crematorium. Cremation then took place behind locked doors.

The Brunners' daughter, Princess Shelagh, did not manage to reach London in time to attend the inquest or the funerals. Three months later she was one of a handful of family mourners when her parents' ashes were interred in Lyne churchyard, to rest near to the grave of Roscoe's father, Sir John Brunner.

Chapter 14

OVER seventy years later, and quite by chance in the Brunner Mond town of Northwich, one of the local newspapers published archive material concerning the deaths of Roscoe and Ethel Brunner. The article was no more than a brief summary of contemporary reports and a few older readers reminisced about the tragic turn of events in November 1926. One young man who knew something of the circumstances of the case took particular notice and carefully cut out the article to send to his aunt who was living in the neighbouring Cheshire town of Altrincham. Two weeks later, in the same newspaper, a letter appeared correcting some of the discrepancies in the Brunner report. This letter was signed by a 'Mrs Isabella Hockenhull' and, clearly, the writer possessed an intimate knowledge of what had occurred at Green Cottage all those years before.

Could this possibly be the young maid Bella Scott, the last person to see the Brunners alive? It was certainly too good an opportunity to miss, but I cannot say who was more taken aback when I telephoned Mrs Hockenhull; she that someone was asking for Bella Scott, or me when she replied in the affirmative. Only those who have spent years searching through dusty records, chased interminable, non-productive enquiries and ruminated for hour upon hour over this fact or that possibility, can appreciate the thrill of locating an eye-witness, more so as I had believed all the principals were probably dead.

When we first met in her retirement flat, Mrs Hockenhull (Bella Scott) had just celebrated her 82nd birthday. She was a lovely, kind-hearted lady, gifted with a splendid memory of those far-off days when, in the mid-1920s and barely out of school, she moved to London, to work at Green Cottage as a between-maid for Prince Ferdinand and Princess Shelagh. Bella's innocence of youth meant she was not privy to much of the household gossip engaged in by the more established, older servants. She picked up snippets, but, as she frequently pointed out in our conversations, 'You knew your place!'

The following is a fascinating account of Bella Scott's recollections and, with the exception of a few minor points, the details of that shocking evening at Green Cottage are amazingly accurate when matched against the formal statements made to the police less than two hours after the bodies were discovered.

> We lived in Great Budworth and Belmont Hall was the centre of the village. Everyone worked there and most of those who didn't were employed at Brunner Mond & Company. The Brunners were the gentry and as a girl I used to see them passing by in their car, or their daughter Shelagh Brunner riding out on her horse. She was certainly no beauty – I suppose you might say, a bit nosey. After the 1914-18 Great War, the village peace celebrations were staged in the grounds of Belmont Hall and as I was a maid of honour, it was my duty to present Mrs Ethel Brunner with a bouquet, on the steps of the hall. I remember I wore a mobcap and she told me I had beautiful hair and that I should let it hang down. She was very charming, but I wasn't sure if she was poking fun at

me. When I left school at fourteen, my father went to see Mrs Brunner and I was offered a position as a maid in London, at Green Cottage, with Shelagh Brunner and her husband, the Prince of Liechtenstein. It seemed a very long way and my mother said if I didn't like it I could come back home when I had saved up the one guinea train fare. I did save the fare, but I decided to keep the money. My wages were £12 a year and I was paid monthly. Green Cottage was what you might call these days, a suburban house. It wasn't very large and the servants often wondered why the Prince and Shelagh lived in somewhere quite so small for their standing. But it never bothered them; they were always away.

There was a cook/housekeeper, a housemaid, a parlour maid and myself and when Shelagh's baby, Christopher, was born I became between-maid, helping with normal duties and assisting the nursemaid when required. It wasn't a large domestic staff compared with other households of that time. The Prince and Shelagh liked to live it up and when it was Royal Ascot, or Wimbledon, large hampers would arrive from Fortnum and Mason. They drove a Lagonda and mixed socially in the highest classes, but these were the halcyon days after the 1914-18 war. It was a different world then. The Prince wanted a gentleman's gentleman and Leonard Attwell was appointed; he was ex-Coldstream Guards. The first cook-cum-housekeeper retired and so Attwell's wife, Nellie, came with him to take on those duties.

Almost as soon as the baby was born, the Prince and Shelagh were off on their travels again and Mrs Brunner came to run Green Cottage, also to look after her and Mr Brunner's own move to Roehampton Court. We were very near to Richmond Park and the garden of Green Cottage ran down to Roehampton Court. It was a grand looking mansion. The butler, Harold Dorrington and his wife came from Belmont Hall to live in at Roehampton Court, to organise the furnishings and effects. Holdstock, the chauffeur, and his wife were also there. Holdstock and Dorrington were very friendly.

Green Cottage had a lovely dining room and a lounge opening out onto what we would now call a patio, with an ornamental pool. The house and all the furnishings were rented. Mrs Brunner lived upstairs, almost using it as a bed-sitter. She was an authoress and she liked to give off a certain aura – she said she wanted peace and quiet for her writing. That was Mrs Brunner though. It was said that a lot of her friends used to snigger behind her back about her novels. Not to put too fine a point on it, she was a bit of a bitch and she dominated Mr Brunner who loved her dearly; he let her have all her own way and the money to do it, but then Mr Brunner was a real gentleman. She was always trying to impress and was not well liked.

Mr Brunner suffered with shingles and often forgot things. He had a habit of tapping his forehead and I've heard her say – 'Ros, when you've finished tapping your forehead, I'll get on with my dinner.' She was that type of woman.

On the night of the tragedy, I took up tea to the writing room and later there would have been eggs and mushrooms for Mrs Brunner. They both seemed fine and I returned downstairs. The kitchen, the butler's pantry and the scullery were all underneath the stairs, down a few steps from the ground floor. I was in the kitchen and heard the hall bell go. I went to see who it was and Mr Brunner was there. He said he had been outside to look for the car and would I telephone Holdstock to say he wanted to leave right away.

Holdstock came and I went upstairs. They were a bit startled when I knocked, perhaps preoccupied, but they certainly both answered. Holdstock was waiting in the kitchen and couldn't understand why the 'boss', as he called him, had not come down; he was always so punctual.

(At this point Bella's memory did not precisely tally with her statement to the police, or those of Mrs Attwell and Holdstock. However the discrepancies were of a trivial nature and unimportant.)

Holdstock came back downstairs and he told me to stay in the kitchen whilst he went to fetch the police. I didn't really know what was going on and I don't suppose I really appreciated the seriousness of the situation. Eventually, two detectives arrived and interviewed me in the dining room, right below where it had happened. I don't recall a great deal about what was said but I hadn't heard any gunshots, or an argument. What does stick in my mind is that the police said Mrs Brunner had been wearing a wig and that she really didn't have much hair. Wigs were fashionable and she used to have them laid out like fans; 'transformations' they used to call them. Queen

Mary made them famous. Mrs Brunner had wardrobes full of clothes and hundreds of pairs of shoes. I know I tried a few of them on; she was just my size. When they were closing down Green Cottage, Dorrington's wife gave me a couple of pairs of shoes, but when I took them home to Great Budworth my mother threw them on the fire; she said I wasn't walking round our village in those because everyone would know where they had come from. With all the publicity and the inquest reports, I was quite a local celebrity for a while.

Shelagh and the Prince never lived in Green Cottage afterwards. It was all so sad. Mr Brunner was such a fine man, maybe too much of a gentleman. He had attained status through merit and we all knew that Sir Alfred Mond for one was deeply jealous. Mr Brunner occasionally came to Green Cottage and usually stayed a few hours, but would then return to his apartment at Cavendish Square. He didn't stay overnight very often. I remember on one occasion helping serve a meal and hearing him say, 'Ethel, amalgamation is the workingman's ruin and it will see Northwich in the gutter'. It was all so sad. Ethel Brunner was too easily made the villain.

Two days after the deaths Bella received a telegram from the Coroner's office instructing her to attend the inquest at Wandsworth Baths. Poignantly she kept the telegram throughout her life, neatly folded in a Brunner Mond & Company Golden Jubilee Mug, embossed with the portraits of Sir John Brunner, Dr. Ludwig Mond and Roscoe Brunner.

Chapter 15

Roscoe and Ethel Brunner.

THE late celebrated journalist Cyril Connolly, the inspiration behind James Fox's highly acclaimed Kenyan murder-mystery 'White Mischief', once wrote in the Sunday Times: 'Does it appeal to our vanity, the notion that logic or intuition or knowledge of the human heart can jump to the conclusion which has escaped all the experts and baffled the police? Or is it fear that injustice has been done and the wrong person convicted? Or that a murderer may still be at large? I believe those old teamsters, vanity and curiosity, play the strongest game, and that we all feel we can complete these jigsaws with human pieces'.

As far as the majority of mysteries are concerned Connolly was probably correct, but the Brunner case is different, because, according to the official version of events, there was never a mystery to investigate in the first place. Yet the assumption is as irresistible today, as it was in some quarters at the time, that all was not as it seemed, that the tragedy had everything to do with the haste to fuse four component companies into Imperial Chemical Industries.

Time was not on the side of the founding fathers, Sir Alfred Mond and Sir Harry McGowan, who saw themselves on an Imperial mission, inspired by no less than the British Empire, and they were determined that nothing, absolutely nothing, would stand in their way. The merger was a vast and complex undertaking somewhere in the financial stratosphere, beyond the comprehension of mere mortals, and it was understandable, immersed as they were in their own self-importance, that Mond and McGowan, at first, did not give Roscoe Brunner a thought. But when tragedy struck it was a different matter. The fall-out and the inquest suddenly became a priority, a potential threat to the grand scheme, and the circumstances needed to be managed and concealed as quickly as possible.

Fortunately, the coroner was so obsessed with the behaviour of the Press that he offered a straight bat as wide as a broadsheet newspaper. He was not interested in looking beyond the obvious and bland verdicts of murder and suicide served to conveniently sidestep the root cause, just as the Daily Mail predicted on the morning of the inquest: 'Whether the whole story will be revealed at the inquest depends upon the course the coroner decides to adopt. He may not consider it necessary, or desirable, to go into matters which, it is understood, involve questions of high finance, the necessity for the rearrangement of the board of control of a great firm, and the payment of a sum stated to be more than £1 million.'

In the accusatorial system of justice practised in England it is for the prosecution to prove guilt beyond a shadow of doubt. Inquest proceedings are different. The arguments are not tossed around in a battle of wits between opposing counsel and the choice of witnesses and evidence rests entirely with the coroner who is tasked with establishing identity, ascertaining the circumstances of how a deceased person came by his, or her, death, and so deliver a verdict. Little has changed since the Brunner case except, from 1926, the majority of inquests now take place without a jury and proceedings are normally adjourned to allow the police more time to conduct further enquiries, including, if relevant, factors from years earlier. By a matter of weeks the Brunner inquest came under the old rules and the coroner, Mr Ingleby Oddie, had no intention of delving into the background, or examining the Brunner deaths within a wider context. He was not as impartial as he should have been and, as he was perfectly entitled, chose the path of least resistance. As a consequence the inquest evidence was watered down and distorted.

But what if, purely hypothetically, Roscoe Brunner had not turned the gun on himself and he had stood before the Central Criminal Court charged with murder, on trial for his life? What mitigating circumstances would a shrewd and perspicuous advocate have pleaded beyond, on the shakiest of opinion, that Brunner was a sick man and not responsible for his actions?

The key would, most certainly, have been to demonstrate a spectacular fall from business eminence, that the defendant had previously been the unchallenged and highly respected chairman of a family business, an international company set fair for further decades of success, prosperity and expansion. None had reason to complain, least of all shareholders who were reaping rich dividends. Then in 1923, on the rebound from a collapsing political career, Sir Alfred Mond returned to the boardroom primed for a coup d'état and, if necessary, betrayal. The sole obstacle in his way was Roscoe Brunner and when Mond slipped effortlessly into his shoes he then raced into a headlong gallop to forge I.C.I.. The end may have justified the means, but it destroyed over half a century of Brunner Mond's proud independence.

These were underlying circumstances, the pathway to tragedy, although it is a matter of opinion whether a clever advocate would have actually saved Roscoe Brunner from the gallows.

Regrettably, from an investigative point of view, there wasn't a trial and no court transcripts, just an inquest, and a heavily stage-managed one at that. Criminal trials leave behind a plethora of archived facts and information, rich hunting ground for the researcher, whereas historic inquest proceedings tend to be barren wastelands and, from the beginning of this investigation, it was frustratingly obvious the official files would be meagre fare, and hard to come by at that.

One possibility rested with Ingleby Oddie's personal files, but this was an exceedingly slim chance as, prior to 1927, coroners were not legally obliged to retain inquest documents. During retirement in the 1930s Ingleby Oddie wrote a book about some of his most noteworthy cases, but the Brunner inquest did not feature, and the Coroners' Office, in Battersea, confirmed it did not hold any of his papers. Everything therefore depended on the Metropolitan Police and preliminary enquiries soon threw up a totally unexpected twist. The Brunner case file – an investigation into what the police and coroner downgraded to a straightforward domestic tragedy – had been locked away for one hundred years, originally stamped to remain closed until the 21st century. This was surprising to say the least, especially when compared with a list of other contemporary violent crimes, including a woman's murder in a railway carriage in Hackney, and the murder of three children in Barnes, both files closed in 1927 for thirty years. So what was it about the Brunner file? Why was it outside the public domain until 2026, when even Cabinet papers relating to the Second World War and King Edward VIII's abdication were open?

I soon established that the Metropolitan Police held responsibility for recommending the extent of closure periods, and most long outdated case files had passed many years ago to the National Archives at Kew. Here it was confirmed, apparently due to 'sensitivity', that the Brunner file was retained in the 'Hundred Years' class, a restriction reduced during the 1970s to seventy-five years. This meant I still could not examine the file and I was left to resort to, then, new Freedom of Information rules. Finally, one has to say 'under pressure', the file was released and the first oddity was the title, flagged on the cover as 'Murder of Ethel Mond and suicide of Roscoe Mond', a simple 'error' apparently, but only recently corrected.

The inquest proceedings referred to in this book are principally from the police transcripts, extensively cross-checked against reports in the London Times and other national, regional and local newspapers which, in those days, were exceedingly more accurate and verbatim in their reporting, especially of high-profile proceedings. Most everything exists one would expect in the yellowing, rather pedestrian Brunner file. Witness statements, including those taken at Green Cottage on the night of the deaths, make up the bulk of the papers and there are newspaper cuttings, a report of the inquest and assorted correspondence, but there is neither photographic evidence (referred to at the inquest) nor post mortem report. It was strange, as if the file had been 'weeded' of sensitive information, a procedure apparently well known to professional researchers who claim material is sometimes burnt or shredded before files are released.

Definitely missing from the Brunner file was a letter submitted ten years after the tragedy by a Mr J.H. Patterson. The only reference to this appears as an irritable, dismissive note scribbled in the file margin: 'It is rather ridiculous that the writer should bother the police with an enquiry such as this, but we have the information and it is common knowledge, and we might say that the late Mr Roscoe Brunner was found shot at Roehampton.'

During my initial research, J.H.Patterson proved to be an elusive, shadowy figure, perhaps even a crank, and his true connection with the case did not surface until years later. He turned out to be John Henry Patterson, an enigma in his own right and far closer to the Brunners than I could ever have imagined. A military man, explorer, author and a major figure in the Zionist movement, Patterson was Britain's official game warden in East Africa prior to the First World War. His duties included accompanying aristocratic tourists on safari and on these expeditions wife-swapping was apparently as popular as big game hunting. In February 1908 Patterson set off to hunt lion with an English gentleman, the Hon. Audley Blyth and his wife Ethel (known to all as 'Effie'). According to Patterson and

J.H.Patterson.

Effie, Blyth went to his tent in the middle of the Ugandan wilderness and shot himself. Patterson and Effie buried the body and continued on their expedition and when they eventually returned to England there were rumours of murder and an affair.

A compelling tale it was later taken up by Ernest Hemingway, 'The Short Happy Life of Francis Macomber', and in 1947 made into a popular film, 'The Macomber Affair', starring Gregory Peck and Joan Bennett.

The Brunner connection? Effie Blyth was Roscoe Brunner's half-sister, the youngest daughter of Sir John Brunner and his second wife Jane Wyman. When Roscoe and Ethel Brunner married in 1898 Effie was one of the bridesmaids and following the Ugandan incident they took her under their wing until she emigrated to New Zealand.

The Metropolitan Police obviously viewed Patterson as a nutcase, but was he? By the time of his letter Effie was dead – she died in 1931 – and this may explain why he waited so long before sending his missive. Did Effie, and therefore Patterson, know something different about the Brunner deaths? Because whatever he was suggesting it is extremely disconcerting the letter has vanished from the official file.

Chapter 16

IN CHARGE of the Brunner investigation was a rather staid, unimaginative plodder, 44-year-old Detective Inspector Albert Eve, a bookbinder by trade who had joined the Metropolitan Police in 1902. He was certainly no Hercule Poirot but, on the evening of Wednesday November 3, 1926, he was the duty inspector when detectives were called to investigate two sudden deaths in a relatively modest dwelling in Roehampton. It was slightly unusual in that two people lay dead, but otherwise, in London, it was fairly routine and, within a few hours, Eve was dispatching a telegram to his Assistant Chief Constable, declaring the matter 'undoubtedly murder and suicide'. There was not a lot more to say and, as there was no need for Scotland Yard to assign a more senior officer to head the enquiries, Eve and his underlings were left to mop up the formalities. All they required was to establish a motive, but to this end neither the servants nor Sir Jack Brunner were particularly helpful, and the police were still floundering when dawn broke to a posse of journalists encamped outside the gates to Green Cottage.

Eve's 'domestic' had suddenly erupted into a full-blown national sensation and everybody was demanding answers, not least the coroner who had already scheduled an inquest for the following Monday. The police were desperate for a break, something to hang their hats on, and this came within twenty-four hours when Sir Jack

Brunner confirmed Press speculation that his sister-in-law's visits to Fleet Street had sparked the tragedy. This was entirely circumstantial but the police seized on it and Det. Insp. Eve was soon telling journalists: 'There is no doubt, or very little doubt, that Mrs Brunner's endeavours to enlist the newspapers for the purpose of airing her grievances, in all probability, incensed Mr Brunner beyond further endurance.'

That was it, done and dusted. Motive? Spontaneous anger without premeditation. The police were satisfied and under the time constraints they had no intention of probing into some of the suspicious anomalies they must have known existed:

(i) Dr Althestane Nobbs, the police surgeon, told the inquest: 'The thing that struck me most was that the drawer, against and under which their heads were, was open. It must have been opened by someone. I asked if anyone had opened the drawer, no-one had. It seemed curious to me that this should be. With the drawer open some nine inches above, it would have been virtually impossible for the bodies to have finished in the position in which they did.'

Apparently the open drawer could be identified on the crime scene photographs, but the coroner and the police were not the least interested in the doctor's observation. Yet someone was not telling the truth. Four people, Nellie Attwell, Thomas Holdstock, Harold Dorrington and Sir Jack Brunner, had all entered the death room before detectives and the police surgeon arrived, and they each had the opportunity to open the drawer. Nellie Attwell, the panic-stricken housekeeper can surely be discounted and Sir Jack Brunner remained under the watchful eye of PC Whitwell who guarded the murder scene. But what of Holdstock and Dorrington?

Trusted members of staff employed by the Brunners for years their behaviour was strange, both before and after the bodies were discovered. Holdstock spent most of his time as Ethel Brunner's personal chauffeur, a capacity in which he enjoyed what may best be described as a privileged, but fiery relationship. In the servants' quarters the gossips said if anyone knew how to handle their temperamental mistress it was Holdstock. On numerous occasions Mrs Brunner had dismissed and immediately reinstated him and, as he was always short of money, would smooth over their disagreements by advancing part of his wages.

Harold Dorrington's position as butler-valet demanded a quieter, more reserved disposition and he too had become a staff fixture at Belmont Hall, transferring to Roehampton Court to assist with the London move. When the unexpected telephone call came through that Mr Brunner required to be immediately conveyed back into the city, Holdstock and Dorrington were both at Roehampton Court, settling down to tea with Holdstock's wife. In his statement to the police, Dorrington said he decided to accompany the chauffeur and 'the boss' 'for the ride', an odd arrangement to say the least. He also stated he had accompanied the chauffeur into the death room when the housekeeper called out and yet neither Holdstock nor Mrs Attwell made mention of this.

Holdstock told the police: 'I went up, entered the writing room, and there saw Mr and Mrs Brunner lying on the floor at the foot of the bed… When I saw Mrs Attwell I said, 'It's finished'. Mrs Attwell then went for the police.'

As we know, the housekeeper came upon PC Whitwell directing traffic almost half a mile away and whilst they were making their way back to Green Cottage Holdstock appeared in the Daimler. Again there was no mention of Dorrington. Where was he? What had they both been up to during the ten minutes it took Mrs Attwell to find a policeman and then set off back to Green Cottage?

There is another baffling question here and though there isn't a textbook guide as to how one should react when confronted with such an horrific scene, why did Holdstock and Dorrington not use the house telephone to alert the police rather than allow Mrs Attwell to scurry off into the night? They certainly managed to contact Sir Jack Brunner who arrived at Green Cottage shortly after PC Whitwell. And what, exactly, are we to imply from the housekeeper and the maid both recalling, on discovery of the bodies, that Holdstock said, somewhat oddly, 'It's finished'?

(ii) Dr Nobbs had a further crucial observation: Ethel Brunner's body was found lying face down, more or less on her stomach, with her husband on his left side, his right arm encircling her waist and his right hand trapped beneath her hip. Brunner still clutched the revolver, a fact attributed to muscle stiffening known to occur in the forearm and hand at the moment of violent death. The police were in no doubt the final position of the bodies was due to 'post mortem movement' and this was probably correct, but that said it all seemed rather neat, almost set-up. Romantically inclined servants had their own take – 'Mr and Mrs Roscoe were together in love to the end, inseparable'.

(iii) Ethel Brunner's 'black eyes'. This was indicative of a violent argument and it begs the question as to why Holdstock and Dorrington, as they told the police, did not hear anything untoward as they dutifully waited with the car beneath the writing-room window? Were they being truthful, or given that it was a cold November night were they, in fact, warming themselves around the kitchen stove? Bella Scott, the maid, was unable to remember seventy-five years later, but from within the basement kitchen, two floors down, she was certain sounds from the bedrooms would not have been detected.

(iv) Many details are profoundly hard to swallow and the most intractable involves Roscoe Brunner's revolver. According to the police and coroner he carried the weapon for the sole purpose of taking his own life: 'He had brought the revolver to London surely not with the intention of killing his wife, but with the intention of killing himself.'

Licensed in Northwich to carry a gun with two-hundred rounds of ammunition, Brunner was the registered owner of a tiny nickel-plated, five-chambered .32 calibre Smith & Wesson a safety-first hammerless model, designed to be quickly removed from a pocket for self-protection and fired at close range. In Cheshire he had always kept the weapon in a small white medicine cabinet at Belmont Hall but over many years it had fallen into disrepair and, in early July 1926, he personally delivered it to Holland and Holland Ltd, gunsmiths in Bond Street, London. Here it was cleaned, put back into action and returned to Belmont Hall. The police found thirteen cartridges and cleaning equipment in a locked drawer at the Cavendish Square apartment though they didn't bother to establish why Brunner had thought it necessary to take the revolver for repair. In July 1926 he was high on optimism that his business career was about to be resurrected in London. The last thing on his mind was suicide.

The police jumped to a hasty conclusion that Brunner was planning to take his own life, because if this was, indeed, the case why would he have chosen to do so at Green Cottage, rather than in the privacy of his own apartment? It doesn't make sense, especially when set against police reasoning that until sitting down with his wife at Green Cottage he was totally unaware of her visits to the newspapers.

When the revolver is placed in a different context there is a more plausible explanation. Brunner had owned the revolver for many years, for the sole purpose of self-protection, and London had probably heightened his concerns. Indeed, it was well known that gentlemen would carry a weapon to defend themselves on the violent streets of those times. The police should have interviewed Alfred James Robinson, Roscoe Brunner's valet who had remained in Cheshire to oversee the closing down of Belmont Hall. I interviewed Robinson's daughter, Mrs Ivy Pickup, of Northwich, who stated that her father had received a telephone call from Mr Brunner instructing him to procure the revolver from the Belmont Hall medicine cabinet and dispatch it immediately to London. Robinson did exactly as he was bid and, with ancillary equipment, the tiny weapon was put on the first available London train out of the local mainline station near to Northwich. The timing is hazy but Mrs Pickup felt sure her father received the telephone call 'not much more than a day before the tragedy'. If correct, this slants towards suicide in Brunner's mind, but if the call was earlier than Mrs Pickup was led to believe then self-protection has to be considered. Police inertia – or was it incompetence? – left the question unresolved.

(v) The untidiness of the writing room: None of the servants were asked to comment on this either in their statements or at the inquest, and yet PC Whitwell remarked: 'There were notes everywhere'. Dr Nobbs also noticed, but, as the servants knew only too well, Ethel Brunner was overbearingly fastidious about the neatness of her living quarters, especially her private papers. And nor was she the type of woman to sit meekly by if her husband, or anyone else for that matter, was plundering her belongings, and this leads to the obvious assumption that a frantic search occurred after her death.

(vi) The most intensely revealing evidence concerns Ethel Brunner's hat and coat she was wearing at the moment she was murdered. In her police statement Bella Scott was adamant she had placed Mrs Brunner's outdoor garments on the hall-stand and her recollection of this remained vivid decades later: 'I remember taking Mrs Brunner's hat and coat when she came in and she was certainly not wearing them when I took up the tea about half an hour later. She didn't come downstairs again and, anyway, the hat and coat she had been wearing when she came in were still on the hall stand.' Like most women of her day Ethel Brunner always wore a hat whenever outdoors and when promoting her novels she was often photographed in the most stylish creations. However, stressed Bella Scott, Mrs Brunner was not in the habit of wearing a hat indoors and it follows she was getting ready to travel with her husband and the chauffeur into the city. There had not been any incoming telephone calls, no hastily arranged social visits and, unlike Dorrington, she certainly wasn't going for the ride. Exasperated and angry at Roscoe's intransigence, and bearing in mind her previous evening's dalliance at such a late hour, her destination was surely Fleet Street.

The police do not seem to have seriously taken any of these factors into account. They were far too sure of themselves as demonstrated by their failure to call in Scotland Yard's fingerprinting branch. Since the turn of the century new methods of forensic analysis were turning crime detection into a science and finger-printing might just have resolved the mystery of the open drawer and, perhaps, identified whose dabs were on the revolver, because, in addition to 'murder and suicide', there were at least three other possible scenarios:

(•) Ethel Brunner grabbed the revolver and took her own life. Had she not once said she would do away with herself if she ever came down in the world?

(•) Roscoe was about to shoot himself and when Ethel intervened she was killed, accidently. This theory was favoured by the family.

(•) An unknown assailant murdered both of them.
Unlikely, but this cannot be eliminated entirely.

The principal witness at the inquest was, of course, Sir Jack Brunner, a career politician, head of the Brunner clan and about to take his seat on the I.C.I. board. He had much to protect and it was understandable he wanted the shocking affair brought to a swift conclusion, the least said the soonest mended. His brother, he said, had 'loyally accepted' his omission from the I.C.I. board, but how could he have known this? In his statement to the police on the night of the deaths he admitted they had not communicated following the Brunner Mond board meeting of October 25. As we shall see later, there was to be another, more serious, volte-face from Sir Jack who chose his words carefully, almost as if the inquest was running to a pre-arranged script. For instance, when the 'merger' was tentatively mentioned he was quick to correct the coroner. This was merely proposed, he countered, and it would only take place if shareholders agreed. I.C.I. was not once referred to by name and nor, directly, was the Lever affair although, in regard to the latter, Sir Jack claimed his brother had taken responsibility for 'serious business troubles', subtly different to saying he was actually responsible. Sir Jack's evidence on the latter point has never been substantiated and yet historians have always taken it as the reason, the definitive explanation, for Roscoe Brunner's omission from the board of I.C.I. and, subsequently, why he murdered his wife, i.e a mild-mannered, genial gentleman who abhorred violence.

The sympathy of the jurymen and the coroner were certainly with Roscoe, primarily because of Sir Jack's insistence that Ethel's visits to the newspapers had turned his brother's brain. This was pure supposition, but the coroner allowed it to fly under a false flag of logic, as he did the assertion that Ethel damagingly interfered in Roscoe's business affairs. The triumvirate days at Belmont Hall suggest otherwise – he did not discourage her involvement and if she had ever been a hindrance it did not affect his career, or his longevity as an exceedingly successful industrialist.

The coroner might have probed deeper into the circumstances behind the deaths, taken a stronger line with Sir Jack, but on the other hand this was an inquest, not a trial. So Sir Jack was not asked about the the I.C.I. board appointments, or why Roscoe, so late in his career and given his well-known ambivalence towards London, had suddenly uprooted from his beloved Cheshire to start a new life in the capital.

Whatever way one looks it, Sir Jack's evidence buried the tragedy for good. The official findings overwhelmingly hinged on what he had to say, the accuracy of his utterances taken for granted. What a pity the coroner refused to delay the inquest for a few days to facilitate the return from the Continent of Princess Shelagh who really could have shed light on the Lever affair, her father's health and her parents' life-changing move to London.

Just as Mond and Sir Jack Brunner must have hoped, the dust quickly began to settle and the British Press lost interest. However, overseas, many newspapers continued to speculate, their readers spellbound by the tragedy. One of these, the Pittsburgh Press, in Pennsylvania, USA, published a full-page news feature, complete with startling artist's impression depicting Roscoe Brunner, revolver in hand, lying across his wife's body. The newspaper described Ethel Brunner as 'attractive, brilliant, the author of novels'. It went on: 'Mrs Brunner had for some weeks been nagging her husband and bewailing the lowering of his business prestige. She had told her story to editors and various strangers. Strange to say, the only reason discoverable for Roscoe Brunner's tragic act was his annoyance at his wife's continual harping on his business humiliation. That a great millionaire of known ability should kill his wife and for such a reason sounds hardly credible, but they have found no other. It is admitted that his wife's talking had done him no substantial injury.'

Overall the article was not entirely accurate, but at least the Pittsburgh Press hit the nail on the head. It was, indeed, 'hardly credible' that Ethel Brunner had simply talked her way to a violent death.

Full page article from the Pittsburgh Press.

Chapter 17

TRAGEDY had been in the making for the best part of three years but it only began to unravel at the critical Brunner Mond board meeting of October 25, 1926. Top of the agenda was confirmation of Sir Alfred Mond's choice of three directors to join him on the twelve-strong board of I.C.I., his son Henry Mond, J.G.Nicholson and G.P.Pollitt, all of whom had accompanied him on the United States' trip and were party to the drawing up of the Aquitania Agreement. Nicholson, an outstanding salesman, and Pollitt, a Brunner Mond technical star, were a fit with Mond and McGowan's demand for big brains and ruthless efficiency, but the appointment of Henry Mond smacked of unadulterated nepotism. Henry, the Johnny-cum-lately, was lined up to be I.C.I.'s director of labour, a position to which Roscoe Brunner was infinitely more suited with his long record of worker/management relations.

What is difficult to fathom, as mentioned earlier, was Brunner's sangfroid as, apparently unfazed, he departed London to regale the Northwich Conservative Association, and even more puzzling was Ethel Brunner's lack of reaction to what most of the staff at Brunner Mond's head office saw as an outrageous snub. How did the embittered wife, this 'impulsive, highly-strung' woman, manage to control her emotions? Why did she wait a whole week before descending on Fleet Street? It doesn't make sense, unless something else was in the offing. Had Sir Alfred Mond reassured his old friend there was still hope, that the appointment of three lay (non-executive) directors was pending, men distinguished in public life, or business, and his guiding voice of wisdom and inspirational leadership over twenty-five years stood him in good stead?

In any event, Brunner returned from Cheshire on Friday October 29 and spent the weekend at Green Cottage with Ethel and their grandson. The servants considered him his normal, imperturbable self, and some remarked on how relaxed the 'Master and Mistress' were as they strolled together in Richmond Park. If the Brunners were anticipating a further announcement then their hopes were soon dashed. On the Monday Brunner returned to /Cavendish Square where he received a copy of the first I.C.I. prospectus, published on that very day. He must have been aghast that his own name was not amongst the chosen, for Mond, who had always been impressed with titles, had selected Sir Jack Brunner, Lord Reading and Lord Ashfield to be the lay directors. Beau Mond, the former Cambridge undergraduate, was playing the greatest poker game of his life and Roscoe Brunner hardly ranked above a deuce.

Sir Jack's appointment was probably the bitterest pill for Brunner to swallow. Hadn't his brother always put political career before the Brunner Mond business and, not a month ago, wasn't he preparing to stand as Liberal candidate in the Northwich constituency? And hadn't he also been one of Mond's acolytes on the United States' trip? What of Lord Ashfield and Lord Reading? Ashfield, a former President of the Board of Trade, had served alongside Mond in the wartime government and both were privy counsellors. Mond was even closer to Reading (Rufus Isaacs). In their early political careers they had sat together on the Liberal benches and then as financiers of the first calibre got themselves entangled with Lloyd George who was accused of insider trading in the notorious pre-war Marconi scandal. Isaacs went on to become Lord Chief Justice and, from 1921-25, Viceroy of India. Elevated to the rank of Marquess, he had recently been casting around for prestigious and remunerative positions and had joined Sir Alfred Mond on the board of the newly-formed Palestine Electric Company. Isaacs' I.C.I. appointment probably came as no surprise to Roscoe Brunner, or to anyone else for that matter. The writing had been on the wall since Mond's Indian holiday and, by Tuesday November 2, the 'former Viceroy' appointment was all over the daily newspapers when they landed on Ethel Brunner's breakfast table.

She was incandescent as the list of directors leapt from the pages: Lord Reading who had neither commercial, nor industrial experience; Lord Ashfield, another of Mond's political allies; Nicholson and Pollitt, both appointed by her husband; Henry Mond, still wet behind the ears, and what did he know about the chemical industry? Sir Jack Brunner, a career politician. Where was Roscoe's name, he who had made such a huge contribution to the success of Brunner Mond?

As she looked back on the chain of events that had brought them to this terrible moment, it was little wonder she snapped. With his late father's blessing Roscoe had managed Brunner Mond through the turbulence of the First World War to a major programme of expansion and acquisition, and it had all been going so well. Her own prestige, the cornerstone of her very existence, had never been greater. She was making a name as a writer, her daughter had married into Royalty, and Roscoe had become the unchallenged head of a prosperous international business. Life could hardly have been better and then Alfred Mond, his political career in abject disarray, had reappeared to claim his seat on the board, and he had then used all his Machiavellian wiles to run rings round Roscoe. What was it Mond said to the Press about the merger? 'Any man in this concern who can prove his value need have no fear that there is not room for him.' Mealy-mouthed words, but when did anyone look for scruples among politicians and, anyway, there was no need to change Brunner Mond. Old Sir John would never have allowed it.

The Lever troubles had effectively done for Roscoe, his only 'crime' to stand by a disgraced colleague and, even if he had made an error of judgement, did he not deserve the benefit of doubt? Mond had made a career out of controversy and he, more than anyone, appreciated the merits of a forgiving second chance. It was so unfair and beyond comprehension that her husband's contribution of decades was being overlooked by fellow directors who had collaborated with Mond to walk all over Roscoe as well as the company's proven paternal style of management.

Mond was an interloper, a novice compared to Roscoe's vast chemical industry experience and impeccable record, and, as a Brunner Mond shareholder in her own right, Ethel demanded to know who had actually given the mandate to merge, to bury Brunner Mond. If there wasn't to be a position for her husband then the merger was odious and contemptible, and if he wouldn't make a fight of it, then she would.

Henry Mond and the Marquess of Reading.

The inaugural I.C.I. board. Sir Alfred Mond and Sir Harry McGowan are in the centre on the front row.

Chapter 18

ETHEL Brunner was no stranger to the media. Eloquent, intelligent and manipulative she had dealt for years in the hard currency of self-publicity to help promote herself and her novels, the Lady Bountiful revelling in celebrity status, expounding her views on all manner of subjects from politics and industrial management to social welfare. She was a prolific writer of articles and letters across the national, regional and local Press of the 1920s, and her wireless broadcasts, 'by Mrs Roscoe Brunner', included such diverse topics as 'Thoughts of London' and 'Education and the Woman'.

The police, the coroner and Sir Jack Brunner perceived her to be an unstable wife who had galloped off to the newspapers in an emotional fit of pique over her husband's humiliating fall from business eminence, but the reality was quite different. She probably knew exactly what she was about when, on the evening of Tuesday November 2, she instructed Holdstock to drive her to the offices of the Daily Herald and the throbbing lights of Fleet Street. Like her eponymous heroine 'Celia' she 'never made a friend or shook hands with a person except with a view to using them for something'.

Any one of seven or eight newspaper offices might have sufficed for a less calculating woman, but Ethel Brunner had good reason to make her first choice the Daily Herald. The official organ of the T.U.C., founded in 1912 by three radicals, one of whom was Ben Tillet, Sir

Alfred Mond's former adversary in Swansea, the Herald was permanently at war with the Conservatives and Liberals, forever campaigning to root out abuse by what it saw as rich and privileged Members of Parliament. Ethel Brunner was certainly no Socialist, more 'right of Genghis Khan', and her Conservative friends would have been mortified that she was pleading her case at what, to them, was a disreputable scandal sheet. However, this lady was not for turning and, at around 8pm, she swept regally into the Herald's reception with a note for the Editor, no less. The following is a fascinating account of that meeting, published in the wake of Ethel Brunner's murder:

> It was one of those hours when visitors are least welcome in newspaper offices. A new edition was well under way. We were all straining in the recurrent race against time. When I was able to spare the few moments asked, I found awaiting me a middle-aged woman, plainly and inexpensively dressed in brown. She was handsome, blonde, blue-eyed, vivacious. Her speech was cultured, and she had a most attractive Irish brogue. Mrs Roscoe Brunner spread on the desk a copy of a financial daily newspaper. She pointed to a story giving particulars of the proposed merging of Brunner Mond & Co., the United Alkali Co., Nobel Industries and the British Dyestuffs Corporation.
> 'Have you noticed anything odd about that?' she queried sharply, almost challengingly. There was in her demeanour no excitement, no hysteria, no hint of impending tragedy. I replied that I had read all the news of the merger.
> 'Don't you see that my husband's name isn't there!' she exclaimed, placing her finger on the list of directors.
> 'He has built up the Brunner Mond business. Old Sir John went into politics and left it to him. His life's work is in it... He has toiled there for 28 1/2 years...'

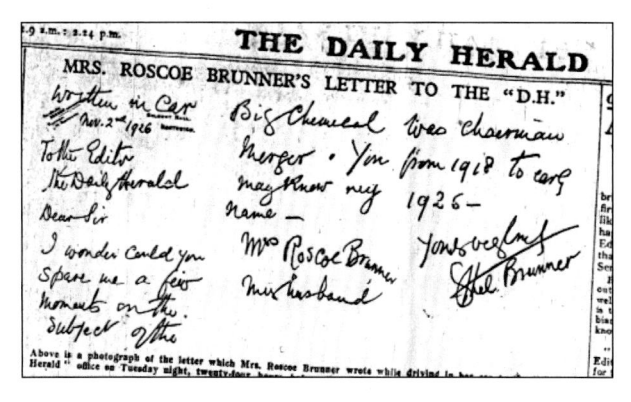

'You may know my name – Mrs Roscoe Brunner.'

By 'Old Sir John' she meant the late Sir J.T.Brunner, Bart. Drumming her foot rhythmically on the floor, Mrs Brunner went on to speak of her husband's scientific knowledge, of her share in his work, of her electing to live in a dreary industrial town when she might have moved in society, and luxuriated on the Riviera.
'We loved our workers!' she declared.
'I'm not concerned only for my husband. I tell you quite frankly I'm not a Socialist. But I feel very deeply about our workers at Northwich. We've done our best to look after them. We've maintained personal touch. Under the merger they are certain to suffer. Combines are soul-less.'
Then she digressed. With a flash of intellectual pride she spoke of her books, adding that she assumed that I had read 'Celia's Fantastic Voyage'. She told me that she was very busy on her new work. 'You must not think that I am a mere literary dilettante,' she continued. 'No-one is more interested in human causes than I am.'
Then from her reticule she drew a pink telegram form.
'Do you see this?' asked Mrs Brunner. 'It's about Spahlinger. That man has found the cure for consumption. I've done all I could to help him.

'What a tragedy!' she exclaimed, her eyes brimming with tears.

'Millions of sufferers, and that great and good man ready with his remedy, but unable to do his work because he has no money.'

Much else she said about her life and, affectionately, about her husband and her family. Now and again she would apologise for occupying my time.

'But what I have to say is so tremendously important! My husband doesn't know I'm here. He is at home, dining on eggs and bacon. He is a man of simple tastes.'

Reverting to the chemical industry, she spoke of the nitrogen fixation factory at Billingham-on-Tees, and of her part in acquiring it cheaply from the Coalition Government.

'There is nothing wrong with the industry,' she declared emphatically. 'It can more than hold its own. The merger is quite unnecessary.'

As we made our way down the stairs to the exit she continued to talk, briskly and vivaciously, about the merger and her husband. Outside was a large motor-car.

'Is that your car?', I asked.

'Yes,' was the reply. 'But I don't know how long it will be ours'. Then she drove off into the fog and the night. What struck me most was that Mrs Roscoe Brunner was labouring under a strong sense of grievance. She was not wildly angry. She was not distraught. She had made up her mind to pursue a certain line at whatever cost to herself. Wifely love and solicitude were obvious in every word of what she said about her husband.

The Night Editor was on his way back to the newsroom when a second note was thrust into his hand. It was, again, from Ethel Brunner and stated simply: 'I thought I would leave my town address and telephone number with you. Many thanks for listening !!!'.

Two hours later she appeared in the plush lobby of a newspaper that was at least in keeping with her Conservative views, the Daily Telegraph. The editor was engaged on more pressing duties and, grudgingly, she agreed to meet with one of the journalists who later wrote:

'Mrs Roscoe Brunner called at the office of the Daily Telegraph within twenty-four hours of the tragedy. She was alone and calm, and displayed no signs of being overwrought. Her conversation was wholly concerned with the affairs of Brunner Mond, and especially the branch of that vast business at Northwich. Her husband, till recent months the chairman, had been chiefly respon-sible, she claimed, for the large increase of the business and establishment at Northwich wherein many thousands of men had been employed and when, throughout the period of the war, the greatest activity had prevailed, day and night, in the manufacture of chemicals required for explosives. Though unemotional, she was evidently moved by a deep-seated sense of grievance that in the constitution of the new board of directors who will control the merger, and whose names had been announced that morning, no place had been found for her husband.'

Ethel Brunner's second note to the Night Editor of the Daily Herald.

Strangely, Ethel Brunner's call at the Daily Telegraph office did not occur until shortly before 11 o'clock, i.e. almost two hours after her visit to the Daily Herald. What had she been up to? Holdstock probably knew, but the police failed to question him and we are left to speculate on several intriguing newspaper references that during Tuesday evening she was involved in an altercation on the doorstep of Sir Alfred Mond's home, in Lowndes Square. According to the reports, she had, apparently, made 'serious allegations', although her wrath could not have been aimed personally at Mond since he was in Northwich, en route to deliver a major speech in Leeds.

Roscoe Brunner was blissfully unaware of his wife's visits to the Herald and the Telegraph. He was dining alone at his Cavendish Square apartment and, according to the steward, William Beldan, he retired at ten o'clock. On the following morning, Wednesday, the last day of his life, he was served tea in bed, breakfasted and then left the apartment. Beldan was absolutely certain the 'boss' did not return and it follows, therefore, that Brunner must have carried the loaded revolver in his pocket throughout the day. This is crucial evidence and it should have prompted the police and coroner to question their own reasoning, namely that he intended to take his own life. Where was the logic when 'self-protection' stared them in the face?

Brunner was a man of routine and his first port of call was the offices of Brunner Mond where he chatted with members of staff who all thought him to be his cheerful and friendly self. This too was the impression of fellow members of the Bath Club when, later, he enjoyed his normal afternoon of conviviality. What seems to have upset the equilibrium was the unexpected, and perhaps embarrassing, appearance of his wife at about four o'clock, insisting he should accompany her to Green Cottage. His friends noted that he appeared a little irritated, but nothing more, and it's doubtful he knew at this point that his wife had already called on the newspapers, or that she was about to present herself at the offices of the Financial News.

At the Financial News offices, in Queen Victoria Street, Ethel Brunner was interviewed by a journalist, William Underhill, who, in the aftermath of the tragedy, summed her up as 'a very level-headed and sound businesswoman'.

Other than the Green Cottage servants, Underhill was the last person to see Ethel Brunner alive, but the police did not bother to interview him. Clearly frustrated, he volunteered an extremely important statement within the context of the tragedy, but, beyond the Metropolitan Police file, this never saw the light of day.

> On Wednesday November 3rd, 1926, in the afternoon, the `Editor was engaged on very private business, which resulted in my attending to some callers. At about 4.30pm one of the messengers brought me in a note addressed in pencil to the Editor, and signed Mrs Roscoe Brunner. She was shown into the office and I greeted her as Mrs Roscoe Brunner. She stated that she would like the help of the journal in order to express her views of the big Chemical Combine (Imperial Chemical Industries Ltd). She deplored the fact that Brunner Mond and Company would lose its individuality by joining the Combine. She stated that for twenty-six years Mr Roscoe Brunner, her husband, had worked very hard in the interests of the company and had done much to build up the company to its present strength. Further, that her husband was the prime mover in projecting the big Synthetic Ammonia Works at Billingham.
> She herself had worked hard together with her husband taking a keen interest in the Brunner Mond enterprise at Northwich, Cheshire. She expressed her surprise and regret that her husband had not been invited to join the Board of the Imperial Chemical Industries, and she could not understand why. She pointed out that Sir Alfred Mond had really only been Chairman for a mere ten minutes – meaning only a

short time – and that now he was handing over this great property to a combine. She said it would have been a great consolation to her and her husband had he been appointed to the Board of the new Company. She felt that he had been ignored, and she intended to get the matter raised in the House of Commons. She stated that as a shareholder, she would appeal to other shareholders to protest against the inclusion of the Brunner Mond interests in the Combine. When I first saw Mrs Roscoe Brunner, I formed the impression that she was somewhat agitated, but during the course of the conversation she grew calmer, and by the time she left my offices she appeared in better spirits... I have never seen Mrs Roscoe Brunner before. She seemed to be very level-headed and a sound businesswoman.

William Underhill was the third journalist to speak with Ethel Brunner and all three had been courteously dismissive, because, intrinsically, there was nothing new in what she had to say and, certainly, nothing to follow up. Nevertheless, she did make several oblique references to Brunner Mond's acquisition of the Billingham-on-Tees chemical facility, and her part in acquiring it cheaply from the coalition government, a topical controversy still causing sparks to fly in the House of Commons.

The final note to the Night Editor of the Daily Herald, as well as her promise to write a letter to the Financial News, indicates her state of mind. She was not done with the newspapers, or Billingham. 'I am in terrible trouble,' she allegedly told a friend on that fateful Wednesday morning. 'I am having the biggest fight I ever had, but I shall win yet!'.

Chapter 19

ETHEL Brunner did know a great deal about the nitrogen plant at Billingham which the government had developed, at enormous cost, during the war to manufacture explosives. The British method, however, seriously lagged behind Germany's Haber Bosch process and, at the end of the hostilities, Britain was determined to get its hands on the secret. A special commission was set up, chaired by Sir Alfred Mond, and a team of boffins, exclusively from Brunner Mond, visited the Haber plant at Oppau, on the Rhine, to effectively steal the secret. Curiously, on their return, the boffins refused to show the blueprint to anyone outside of Brunner Mond and, it seems save to assume, the privileged few included Sir Alfred Mond who was the first to recognise the peacetime potential of the Haber process in the manufacture of fertilisers.

In the aftermath of war Britain was seriously in debt and hardly an eyebrow was raised when, as part of large scale asset-disposal, the government sold the Billingham factory to Brunner Mond, at what turned out to be a ludicrously knockdown price. Brunner Mond then proceeded to create a new subsidiary out of Billingham, the Synthetic Ammonia & Nitrates Company with Roscoe Brunner as its first chairman. Historians have always claimed that Brunner Mond 'reluctantly' purchased Billingham, but this was not necessarily so. The company landed a veritable bargain in acquiring the site and with it the technologically advanced German secret. Moreover, there was to be an 'unexpected' additional treasure when, miraculously, an almost limitless supply of anhydrite, a mineral invaluable for development of the Haber Bosch process, was discovered beneath the Billingham site. Whether this was an incredible stroke of good fortune, or a carefully worked ruse, no-one knew, but Brunner Mond certainly struck gold. The losers were Nobel Industries who were to have shared ownership, but at the last minute, apparently for financial reasons, withdrew from the deal, leaving Brunner Mond to go it alone. The question is, would Sir Harry McGowan and Nobels have pulled out of if they had known of the Haber Bosch potential and the riches about to be unearthed?

As soon as the Billingham sale was confirmed, word began to get out of Brunner Mond's good fortune and many Labour MPs from the North East expressed outrage, accusing the government of collusion to the detriment of the British taxpayer. One who had long felt he could smell a rat was John Beckett, the Labour MP for Gateshead, who persistently pressed for answers. He wanted to know how much the government had invested in Billingham during the war and how much Brunner Mond had paid for the facility. He didn't get very far – 'contrary to the public interest' was the typical lame excuse – and the true figures did not emerge until many years later, long after the affair had been forgotten and I.C.I. was firmly established. These revealed the government had initially invested over £1 million in Billingham and Brunner Mond then paid £715,000 for the facility, including the Haber Bosch secret and the anhydrite.

Beckett never succeeded in getting to the bottom of what had gone on but, supported by his colleagues, he continued to forcibly express his concerns and he was still raising the matter in the House of Commons during the mid-1920s:

As far as I can trace the history of this transaction, the government, after sending a Commission to Oppau, to discover the German method of the fixation of nitrogen, sold the factory which had certainly cost the British taxpayer a very large sum of money, to Messrs Brunner Mond Ltd, at a figure very much below the price which the British taxpayer had been called upon to pay. I want to put to the Minister responsible, who were the members of this Commission? I want to know whether the Chairman of the Commission is now a director of the firm exploiting the Haber process. I want to know if any report was received from that Commission. If such a report was received I want to know when it was received. I should very much like to know, and I am sure that the public would be interested to know, whether the report was received from members of this Commission before or after they left the Government service and entered the service of Messrs Brunner Mond and Company?

I am sure also we should be interested to know whether the report was received by any responsible government department before the sale of the factory under private treaty to Messrs Brunner Mond. In reply to a question the Secretary of State for War said this factory was very widely advertised before it was sold by private treaty, the terms again being against the public interest to disclose. I want to know if, when the factory was advertised, other people knew that the Haber process was being thrown in like a pound of tea.

Beckett's salvoes were aimed at Sir Alfred Mond and his Brunner Mond board colleague, Lt-Col G.H.Pollitt, who had headed the boffins' raid on Germany and who went on to be appointed the first managing director of Synthetic Ammonia & Nitrates Company. Some observers at the time believed Beckett and his Labour colleagues were acting from a vindictive dislike of Sir Alfred Mond, trying to discredit him because of his 'destructive' speeches against Socialism, and, for its part, Brunner Mond issued a denial, effectively claiming it had purchased Billingham in good faith and, in keeping with government wishes, had developed an almost virgin site. The Haber Bosch process and the anhydrite discovery were not mentioned.

The Billingham accusations were still rumbling in 1926, a murky business, and it remains an inescapable fact that Brunner Mond did exceedingly well from Sir Alfred Mond's central role in the acquisition saga. It might also explain a curious entry in Brunner Mond's minutes shortly after his reappointment as a director in 1923: 'Resolved that the common seal of the company be affixed to an agreement with the Rt Hon. Sir Alfred Mond MP for services other than those of an ordinary director…'

'Services other than those of an 'ordinary director'? Did this have anything to do with the Billingham acquisition? Quite possibly, but all we know for definite is that Mond was passionate about the potential for Billingham. Indeed, immediately on succeeding to the chairmanship of Brunner Mond he threw himself into creating a vast plant and a company town over which, it was said, the night sky flamed red with fire and smoke from the belching chimneys of iron foundries and the great chemical works.

Under Brunner Mond, Billingham began to evolve into the evocative face of industrial Britain and it became the inspiration for Aldous Huxley's acclaimed dystopia, 'Brave New World', whose central theme was 'rationalisation' governed by 'the resident world controller of Western Europe', Mustapha Mond (Must-Have-a-World). It has been said in both appearance and nature Mustapha Mond was undoubtedly sculpted from Sir Alfred Mond, '… a man of middle-height, with black hair, a hooked nose, full red lips and piercing dark eyes. Intelligent and learned, (Mustapha) Mond has an acute sense of irony and even a certain sense of humour'.

One who was definitely not thinking about Mond's sense of humour, real or imaginary, was Ethel Brunner when she made her round of visits to the newspapers hinting she had much to say about Billingham, Brunner Mond's jewel in the I.C.I. merger negotiations. Maybe it appealed to her sense of drama, or, more probably, she was holding something back, something guaranteed to arouse media interest, something involving a former government minister, her arch-enemy, Sir Alfred Mond? If this was, indeed, her intention then she would have realised she required substantive evidence, irrefutable documentary proof to convince cynical journalists. Sir Alfred Mond's record in the libel courts was legendary.

Footnote: As well as Huxley's 'Brave New World' Sir Alfred Mond also appears in an enigmatic poem 'A Cooking Egg', published in 1920 by T.S.Eliot: The following is an extract:

>   I shall not want Honour in Heaven
>   For I shall meet Sir Philip Sydney
>   And have talk with Corolianus
>   And other heroes of the kidney.
>
>   I shall not want want Capital in Heaven
>   For I shall meet Sir Alfred Mond:
>   We two shall lie together, lapt
>   In a five percent Exchequer Bond.

Analysts say Eliot chose Mond as typical of a twentieth century enlightened businessman demanding greater units, greater co-ordination, more effective use of resources, mass production and benevolent industrial dictatorship in which the individual is little more than a nonentity in the larger scheme of industrial empire.

Billingham's Brave New World. G.P.Pollitt (below), Managing Director. Right: Sir Alfred Mond with the Prince of Wales at Billingham.

Chapter 20

THE only sure fact in the Brunner tragedy is that two people died in violent circumstances at Green Cottage on the evening of Wednesday November 3, 1926. Everything else is speculation, not so much in regard to the inquest verdicts, which in the long run were probably correct, but the explanation that Roscoe Brunner murdered his wife because she had visited the newspapers to fight their corner. The police had no doubt but, viewed from the distance of decades, it is apparent they were neither tenacious, nor incisive, in their enquiries, and a hasty grope in the dark prevailed in order to set a case before a coroner exasperated by what he regarded as appalling Press intrusion.

So, if one turns the case on its head and considers the whole sorry affair from a different perspective, what could have happened in those final hours? Why did Roscoe Brunner carry his loaded revolver to the rendezvouz with his wife, and had she really played her last card in her efforts to interest the newspapers, Socialist, Conservative and Financial?

'Good night, sir,' calls the doorman of the Bath Club as Roscoe Brunner steps out into the London fog. Uncharacteristically preoccupied with his own thoughts, Brunner does not respond. In Dover Street he purchases the evening's final edition of the London Standard with its headlines screaming that the national coal stoppage may be about to end. Brunner has deeply felt the struggle between worker and management and yet, for the first time in a long and eminent business career, he has been helpless, to intervene or influence.

A large black Daimler pulls alongside and Brunner alights into the back seat to be greeted by his wife as affectionately as any man might expect after over a quarter of a century of married life. On their way to Roehampton the chauffeur, Thomas Holdstock, hears Mr & Mrs Brunner chatting amicably. At the front door of Green Cottage they are greeted by the maid who divests them of their outdoor apparel. Mrs Brunner orders tea to be served in the first floor writing-room that doubles as her private bedroom. The coal shortage impinges on all, even the wealthy.

They climb the stairs, initially to visit the nursery and their baby grandson in the care of his nanny, and by six-thirty they are settled in front of the writing-room fire when the maid, Bella Scott, enters with their tea. Mr Brunner instructs Scott to inform Holdstock that he will be required at eight o'clock, to take him back into the city. Mrs Brunner says she will supper after her husband's departure.

The maid returns to the basement kitchen and the chauffeur takes the opportunity of an hour's break to briefly slip away to his own quarters at nearby Roehampton Court.

In the writing-room the conversation turns to the I.C.I. merger and the board appointments. Brunner has accepted the situation, yielded to circumstances, perhaps lost the will to fight, and he is angered and humiliated when his wife outlines her visits to the newspaper offices. The argument quickly descends into a full-blown row as he tries, and fails, to persuade her to drop the matter. She demands he stand up for himself as the one respected figure capable of swinging Brunner Mond shareholders against Sir Alfred Mond and the merger. Brunner recoils at the thought of his father's company and his own name being used in such a way. He's had enough and he's going back to his apartment at Cavendish Square.

It is now about seven o'clock as he storms from the room to find the chauffeur. In the basement kitchen, Bella Scott hears the hall bell. Mr Brunner is standing at the open front door and instructs her to telephone the chauffeur at Roehampton Court. He is required immediately.

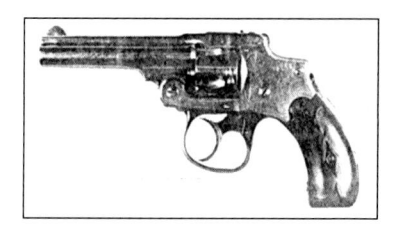

Brunner's five-chambered .32 calibre Smith & Wesson.

Brunner is anxious to avoid further confrontation with his wife, but he, the master, can hardly stand in the hall to await the chauffeur and, reluctantly, he retraces his steps to the writing-room.

His wife is in a state of high dudgeon. She is putting on her hat and coat. She is intending to travel with him into the city. If he is refusing to make a fight of it then she will and, this time, the newspapers are sure to take her seriously. She has documents that will strangle the merger at birth. Brunner is at his wit's end as she outlines the contents.

He loses control and in a fit of exasperation strikes her. Suddenly, there's a knock at the writing-room door, the maid to say the car is ready. Emotions are high and they react as one… 'Don't come in!'.

Scorning her husband's impassiveness, his threats and her swollen face, Ethel Brunner remains determined to leave for Fleet Street, with or without him. He is powerless to stop her and then his hand rests on the tiny, self-protection, revolver concealed in his pocket.

She moves to the writing-desk and he walks behind her. With a single bullet to the side of her neck he snuffs out her life. He then steps over her body and commences a frenzied search to locate the incriminating documents. When he finds it, the most appropriate repository is the writing-room fire. His final act is to kneel, place his left arm around his wife's body and pull the trigger.

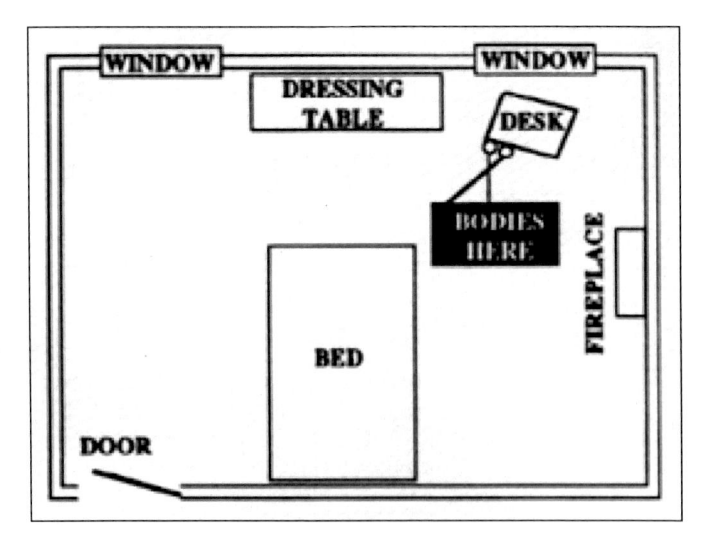

Ethel Brunner's bedroom-cum-writing room where the bodies were found.

Chapter 21

> London Evening Standard:
> Mr Roscoe Brunner, it was said, was willing to take his eclipse, calmly without protest. But not so his wife. She believed she was destined to be her husband's inspiration. She was clever and a successful novelist too. She took her husband's resignation from Brunner Mond as a personal affront which she should put right. She urged her husband to assert himself, but Mrs Brunner's great energy and social pride made her agitate outside their immediate circle.

> Weekly Dispatch:
> Mrs Roscoe Brunner seemed to think the merger was unnecessary and above all that it would hamper the social work she and her husband had done among the firm's tens of thousands of workers. There are some men who resent intensely, and almost furiously, the effort of a wife to control or direct them, who decline, in Stephenson's phrase, to go through life like smiling images pushed from behind. Mrs Brunner, blinded by her love for her husband, quite failed to realise that intrusion and dominance in his business affairs might drive him quite off his mental balance.

THE most unpalatable aspect of an almost universal outpouring of sympathy for Roscoe Brunner was the portrayal of his wife as the villain, that she was a loose-cannon drama queen, a meddlesome, out-of-control woman who had run amok in Fleet Street. The authorities and the Press were content to heap the blame on Ethel Brunner whilst the flint-hearted directors of Brunner Mond, quite deliberately one assumes, failed to acknowledge her at all in their board minute eulogy signed off by the company chairman Sir Alfred Mond: '... the Board of Directors express its most profound and sincere sympathy and condolences with the sons and daughter, and the family of the late Mr Roscoe Brunner in their sad bereavement and wishes to place on record its high appreciation of the devoted and faithful services which he rendered to the Company for a long period of years. The members of the Board all feel a great and personal loss at the passing of an esteemed colleague whom they held in warm and affectionate regard.'

As far as concerned Sir Alfred Mond and the board, Ethel Brunner was an interfering, extreme eccentric opposed to the merger and so the tragedy must have been her fault, her guilt taken for granted, never mind that she was shot in cold blood. She may have been everything they said about her, and more, but it was 'poor Roscoe' who was made out to be the victim, excused for his actions because he was supposedly sick and bordering on suicide.

But was he? Certainly his GP thought him unwell, and yet most everybody else in the final days and hours, considered him to be his relaxed, friendly self – the steward at his apartment, Brunner Mond office staff, fellow members of the Bath Club, the chauffeur Holdstock, the maid Bella Scott, the nurse, Ethel Buckle. If there was a health issue immediately prior to his death it was nothing more than, as reported, a mild bout of influenza.

None of Roscoe Brunner's acquaintances looked at him and thought, here is a man verging on suicide. It was absurd, but the police stacked it so on the flimsiest of evidence, principally because he was carrying a revolver and Ethel had visited various newspapers. The coroner, compelled to show he understood precisely what had occurred, seized on this flawed logic to furnish the jury with a hopelessly inadequate explanation. Members of the public were told nothing the coroner, Sir Alfred Mond and Sir Jack Brunner did not want them to know.

However, not everyone was duped by the official version of events and members of the Green Cottage domestic staff, as well as many friends and acquaintances, were left shaking their heads, convinced the inquest had been a sham. Bella Scott remarked tartly: 'We all knew the reason 'ill-health' was just an excuse.' Meanwhile, draughtsman Jack McCormack, in Cheshire, echoed the thoughts of great swathes of Brunner Mond employees: 'It was felt Sir Alfred Mond had conspired against Mr Brunner.'

Another who strongly doubted the direction and impartiality of the official enquiry was a London psychiatrist, Haydn Brown, who, unlike Sir Jack Brunner, *was* a medical expert to opinionate of matters of mental health, and he could have commented, professionally, on Roscoe Brunner's state of mind. Haydn Brown had been acquainted with the Brunners for over ten years and, clearly, he felt uncomfortable at the public crescendo that had been whipped up against Ethel Brunner. On the day before the inquest, he voluntarily submitted a carefully-worded statement but, like the offering from William Underhill, it was suppressed, lamentably ruled irrelevant by the coroner. Fortunately, a copy of the statement survives in the Police archives. It reads as follows:

The illness of Mr Roscoe Brunner has been repeatedly referred to in the public press, but not the illness of Mrs Roscoe Brunner. She has many friends and relatives who might wish that the latter point should be taken into account, for various reasons. I first made the acquaintance of both ten years ago when Mrs Brunner was suffering from a kind of nervous disorder which is always extremely difficult to deal with. After some months Mrs Brunner recovered and she continued to be well until her husband's business affairs began to cause worry. Anxiety neurosis and intense urge were the main features. A few weeks ago she wrote saying that she would come to London again, to see me. She did not come. She evidently felt that the further worries about business and the new house had better be fought through before she came to see me. Of late Mr Brunner had no power to persuade her on any point whatsoever; his expostulations only aroused her determination to be energetic all the more. I do not consider that Mrs Brunner had a bad temper, as reported. She was captivatingly and cleverly firm, also intensely energetic. Her later relationship with her husband just was quite amicate. She had a high opinion of him; and he of her. The two had arranged to go abroad together on a happy mission before the tragedy.

There was definitely another side to this story, but the coroner wasn't interested and Ethel Brunner was publicly hung out to dry with only the Daily Telegraph proffering the sort of incisive obervation the inquest should have considered: 'Those who knew Mrs Brunner best have little doubt as to the cause of the tragedy. They knew Mrs Brunner would never agree that her husband retired from the chairmanship of Brunner Mond & Company solely through ill-health.'

A further enlightening insight came from an unlikely source, an

'Anonymous friend', who was quoted in the Press on the eve of the inquest. Newspaper 'Anons' must always be treated with suspicion, but this one was particularly well-informed:

> I think I can piece together the circumstances of their mental attitude which culminated in the tragedy. The origin of the trouble, as Mrs Roscoe Brunner explained it to me, may be traced to a business deal that Brunner Mond & Co. had with another great firm. Mr Roscoe Brunner was chairman of his company at the time and, his wife told me, took the whole onus of the transaction on his shoulders. Later he resigned the chairmanship in favour of Sir Alfred Mond M.P.. This occurred during the General Strike and attracted little attention. The severance came as a great blow. Mr Brunner was tremendously proud of his firm. 'My husband and I,' she told me, 'had the choice and ample means to gratify it, of entering into the social life of London, but for the sake of the business, we preferred to bury ourselves in Northwich and take charge of the business on the spot'. Mrs Brunner was continually urging her husband to fight for recognition as one who had worked so hard at the head of Brunner Mond & Company, and went so far as to press him to challenge his company's actions in joining the combine. 'No-one will ever know,' she often emphasised to me, 'how I, a mere woman, helped him in his great efforts.'

The coroner had his own reasons, of course, for not permitting the proceedings to stray a jot beyond the required formalities, i.e. to bring the matter to a comforting conclusion and spike further Press speculation and, therefore, he was content to sit back and allow Ethel Brunner to be condemned. Nobody spoke for her – nobody was allowed to speak for her – and goodness knows what purpose Sir Travers Humphreys served as he, supposedly, represented 'Mrs

Brunner's family' but failed to make a single noteworthy utterance. Everything pointed in one direction and the wise man and the fool took that direction, including the coroner, the police and most of the newspapers. Ethel Brunner took the rap and it's a stigma that has been attached to her name for almost a century.

The 'evidence' against her – visits to the newspapers – was ridiculously wafer-thin, so who actually made her the scapegoat? As ever we must return to Sir Alfred Mond and the I.C.I. merger. Ethel Brunner had always held a radically different view over the future direction of Brunner Mond and, as far as concerned the merger, Mond definitely considered her a dinosaur. The last thing he needed at the most sensitive moment in the I.C.I. negotiations was a scandal to threaten the merger which, as he later admitted, was far from certain: 'We could not form a definite, or conclusive opinion as to how far the shareholders would accept the invitation to exchange their shares – we had to take a certain amount of risk.'

At personal level Mond was also trying to wring a Viscountcy out of Prime Minister Stanley Baldwin, an honour, he said, 'to protect his international responsibilities in the business world'. Additionally, according to his biographer, there was a degree of self-enrichment in Mond's thinking as he was determined to build himself a £15

Roscoe's brother – Sir Jack. John Fowler Leece Brunner.

million fortune to fulfil a promise to help Jewish people return to Palestine. I.C.I. was to be his rainbow's crock of gold.

No-one was ever more sure of himself than Sir Alfred Mond but the Brunner deaths shocked him to the core and when the news broke in Cheshire he was on the first train back to London, to manage whatever collateral damage might come his and I.C.I.'s way. He sat in the shadows, but his influence was all over what turned out to be a cleverly orchestrated cover-up. A politician of twenty years he was a master when it came to pulling strings amongst London's ruling elite, the masonic lodges of the Square Mile, the chummy old boys who protected their own. It was all about averting attention from I.C.I., sowing disinformation and diluting what, overnight, had become a national sensation. The police and the coroner he could personally handle but, as any spin doctor worth his salt would have told him if he didn't know already, the first priority was control of the Press hounds baying at the door. To this end, a meeting was hastily convened with Sir Jack Brunner who emerged to inform reporters that his brother had been a sick man, and, by inference, not responsible for his actions. He did not mention his sister-in-law, Brunner Mond or I.C.I., but the 'sick man' revelation was a new line and the Press lapped it up, so that by the following morning, Friday November 5, every national newspaper was linking Roscoe Brunner's health with Ethel's Fleet Street forays.

Later at the inquest Sir Jack confirmed the connection and with two and two making five the coroner dressed up the newspaper accounts for his own summary and merely endorsed what the public had already been told. In doing so he astonishingly failed to consider an utter contradiction in Sir Jack's evidence. In his statement to the police at Green Cottage on the night of the tragedy, Sir Jack said his brother had been in 'good health', although 'bad last year with shingles'. Fourteen hours later, immediately following the damage-limitation meeting with Mond, Sir Jack changed his mind... Roscoe was a 'sick man' teetering on the verge of a mental breakdown!

A few days before the inquest and at his own instigation, Sir Alfred Mond, the chairman of Brunner Mond and self-appointed voice of I.C.I., arranged an audience with the coroner, a fellow Edinburgh University graduate with whom he was well acquainted, and the only possible reason must have been to keep his own name and that of I.C.I. out of the inquest proceedings.

The Daily Herald speculated: 'In view of repeated references to the late Mr Roscoe Brunner's association with chemical industry finance it is considered probable that a witness will be Sir Alfred Mond, chairman of Imperial Chemical Industries – the merger of which Mrs Roscoe Brunner spoke when she visited the newspapers.'

The Herald was wrong. The private tête-à-tête had served its purpose. Mond had struck at the coroner's Achilles heel in stressing that the presence of a former government minister was bound to fuel a further round of sensational reporting. The I.C.I. merger was at the heart of the tragedy, pivotal to the entire investigation, but Mond was allowed to stay well clear. The police did not bother to interview him; he wasn't called as a witness and, in fact, did not even attend the inquest. It seems he had a more pressing personal matter. On Monday November 8, the day of the inquest, he is recorded as attending the Lady Margaret Freemasons' Lodge, London, where he formally passed into the 'Fellowcraft', the second stage on the ladder of Freemasonry. He was subsequently raised to a Master Mason, in February 1927, and until his death remained a member of both the Lady Margaret and Old Cheltonians Lodges.

Another in the Establishment inner-circle was Brigadier General Sir William Horwood, the Metropolitan Police Commissioner, who, during the first days of the investigation, was also on Mond's need-to-see list, someone else he needed to influence. Immediately after the inquest Horwood received the following note from Mond:

> My dear Sir William
> I should like to convey to you my sincere thanks for the great kindness which we have received from Superintendent Hawkins and Detective-Inspector Eve over the Inquest yesterday. Both Superintendent Hawkins and Detective Inspector Eve were most helpful in every way, and as Chairman of Brunner Mond & Coy. Ltd., and of the Imperial Chemical Industries Limited, I would like to thank you and ask you to be kind enough to convey our thanks to them.
> Alfred Mond

The note is odd since Mond was not a member of the family, and he had gone out of his way to distance himself from the entire affair. But then, his avuncular hand and influence was everywhere. As one sceptical servant observed: 'It's good to be rich and powerful'.

IMPERIAL CHEMICAL INDUSTRIES LIMITED.

Authorized Capital - - £65,000,000.

DIRECTORATE:

The Right Honourable Sir ALFRED MOND, Bart., P.C., M.P. (Chairman).
Sir HARRY McGOWAN, K.B.E. (President and Deputy Chairman).
The Right Honourable the LORD ASHFIELD, P.C.
Sir JOHN BRUNNER, Bart.
G. C. CLAYTON, Esq., C.B.E., M.P.
H. J. MITCHELL, Esq.
HENRY MOND, Esq.
Sir MAX MUSPRATT, Bart.
J. G. NICHOLSON, Esq.
Lt.-Col. G. P. POLLITT, D.S.O.
The Most Honourable the MARQUESS OF READING, P.C., G.C.B., G.C.S.I., G.C.I.E., G.C.V.O.
Sir JOSIAH STAMP, G.B.E.
B. E. TODHUNTER, Esq.

Secretary:
J. H. WADSWORTH.

Treasurer:
W. H. COATES, LL.B., B.Sc.(Econ.)

BANKERS:
BARCLAYS BANK, LIMITED, 54, Lombard Street, London, E.C.3.
LLOYDS BANK LIMITED, 42-4, Gracechurch Street, London, E.C.3.
MIDLAND BANK LIMITED, 5, Threadneedle Street, London, E.C.2.
NATIONAL PROVINCIAL BANK LIMITED, 15, Bishopsgate, London, E.C.2.
WESTMINSTER BANK LIMITED, 41, Lothbury, London, E.C.2.

SOLICITORS:
CLIFFORD-TURNER, HOPTON & LAWRENCE, 61-67, Gresham Street, London, E.C.2.
SLAUGHTER & MAY, 18, Austin Friars, London, E.C.2.

BROKERS:
LONDON: W. GREENWELL & CO., 2, Finch Lane, E.C.3.
HESELTINE, POWELL & CO., 1, Drapers' Gardens, E.C.2.
SHEPPARDS & CO., Gresham House, Old Broad Street, E.C.2.
LIVERPOOL: ASHTON, TOD & NOBLE, 7, Tithebarn Street.
HORNBY, TOBIN & OCKLESTON, 3, Tithebarn Street.
T. & T. G. IRVINE, 3, Rumford Street.
MANCHESTER: W. A. ARNOLD & SONS, 34-35, Haworth's Buildings, Cross Street.
BIRMINGHAM: FYSHE & HORTON, 3, Temple Row West.
BRISTOL: H. C. WOODCOCK & CO., 39, Nicholas Street.
CARDIFF: LIDGETT GIBBS & CO., 50, Mount Stuart Square.
LEEDS: TENNANT & HIRST, Commercial Buildings, Park Row.
SHEFFIELD: HART, MOSS & CO., 14, Norfolk Street.
NEWCASTLE-ON-TYNE: WISE, SPEKE & CO., 53, Grey Street.
EDINBURGH: BELL, COWAN & CO., 22, St. Andrew Square.
GLASGOW: KERR, ANDERSONS, DUNN & CO., 45, Renfield Street.
BELFAST: ARTHUR D. MacILWAINE & CO., 1, Wellington Place.
DUBLIN: DUDGEON & SONS, 113, Grafton Street.

AUDITORS:
THOMSON McLINTOCK & CO., 71, Queen Street, London, E.C.4.
PRICE, WATERHOUSE & CO., 3, Fredericks Place, London, E.C.2.

Registered Office and Transfer Office:—
Broadway Buildings, 50/64, Broadway, Westminster, London, S.W.1.

Secretarial and Administrative Office:—King's Buildings, Smith Square, London, S.W.1.

The only director from outside the four merging companies was the Marquess of Reading. His appointment was publicly announced on the very day Ethel Brunner commenced visiting the newspapers.

Chapter 22

OVER and done with in less than a week, an almost impenetrable veil fell over the Brunner deaths. The coroner cleared his desk to prepare for the next tragedy, the police archived their files, and journalists, bound by a never-ending quest for sensationalism, turned their attention to new headlines and the disappearance of the crime novelist Agatha Christie. Sir Alfred Mond's shadowy role, the £multi-million I.C.I. merger, the archives locked away for a hundred years, nothing quite squared and never was this more apparent than on the evening of the funerals.

Forbidden from attending the funeral service, Green Cottage's knot of staff decided to lock up and visit a local public house, to raise a glass to the memory of Mr and Mrs Brunner. Absent for only a few hours they were stunned on their return to discover the property had been burgled. But this was no ordinary burglary, far from it.

The police arrived in force under the supervision of none other than the intrepid Det. Insp. Albert Eve who quickly established that access had been gained via the drawing-room window. Two sets of footprints were found in the bushes and he surmised the burglars must have hidden themselves until the servants had left for the pub. Inside, the footprints continued across the drawing-room into a passage and then up the stairs to the death room, a clear indication the intruders knew the layout of Green Cottage. Their sole target was

Ethel Brunner's bureau and this had been ransacked to leave jewellery, cheque books, letters and documents scattered across the floor and bed. Eve admitted to being utterly baffled over motive but dismissed as 'irrelevant' the fact that the room was in the same disarray as noted by two of his colleagues on the night of the tragedy. His best guess was that 'ghoulish opportunists' had been responsible, that they were searching for documents connected with Spahlinger's tuberculosis clinic, a notion later dismissed by the doctor himself. Eve felt sure amateurs were responsible since not the slightest care had been taken to conceal footprints or fingerprints which, with far more diligence than in his enquiries into the Brunner deaths, he called on forensics to investigate.

> **BURGLED ROOM OF DEATH**
> **NEW SENSATION IN BRUNNER TRAGEDY.**
> **Search for Letters.**

It didn't help and there were more questions than answers. The only clue came from a neighbour who had observed 'two heavy-overcoated men' driving away in a motor-car at about 9.30pm. Two other witnesses reported lights in the house at around 9pm.

The News of the World was one of the first to pick up on what it described as an 'amazing and lamentable outrage': 'A tool like a jemmy was used to force the drawers. Every paper seems to have been examined, and old bills and cheques were found by the police scattered about near the foot of the bed. They seem to have made a hurried flight, for the condition in which the bedroom was found suggests that their search became frantic as time went on and the possibility of the servants returning grew greater.'

Amongst theories advanced to account for the raid, the News of the World's advanced two possibilities: (i) The burglars were looking for a pearl necklace Ethel Brunner had been wearing on the night of her death. (ii) They were endeavouring to secure letters received by Mrs Brunner shortly before her death.

The latter intriguing hypothesis was also put forward by the London Evening Standard: 'It is believed there were documents at Green Cottage which may have contained Mr Brunner's answer to the suggestions which led to his removal from the chairmanship of Brunner Mond. These documents were never found.'

The servants, meanwhile, had their own suspicions, as outlined by Bella Scott. The chauffeur and butler, Holdstock and Dorrington, failed to appear at the pub until much later than the others and, afterwards, it was surmised the pair were responsible for the break-in, trying to recover iou's that Ethel Brunner held against advances on their wages. Bella Scott recalled: 'Holdstock and Dorrington were as thick as thieves – but you never knew quite what they were up to and the others thought they broke in so they wouldn't have to pay money back when Shelagh returned.'

The riposte to this must surely be that any iou's would already have attracted the attention of the police and Sir Jack Brunner. Fur-

---

NEW BRUNNER SENSATION

"Amateur" Burglars Leave Valuables Untouched

HUNT FOR PAPERS

No Care Taken to Hide Finger-prints

A burglary with the puzzling and startling feature that only papers or documents were sought for has once more brought into prominence the ill-fated Green Cottage at Roehampton, where Mr. and Mrs. Roscoe Brunner were found shot last week.

One room only was entered, the bedroom where the shooting actually occurred. Such silver articles as were there were simply littered on the floor, but drawers and bureau were thoroughly ransacked.

The police inquiring into the matter yesterday were of the opinion that the burglars were amateurs, but knew the cottage well.

thermore, if Holdstock and Dorrington were in such pecuniary straits as to stage a daring raid, wouldn't they have snatched the odd trinket? Holdstock and Dorrington cannot be entirely eliminated, but they were definitely back in Cheshire when a second, even more startling burglary occurred four months later.

The Prince and Princess were living elsewhere in London, the servants had left and Green Cottage was being watched over by a part-time caretaker who, on his routine early-morning round, discovered a rear door forced and, just as on the night of the deaths and the night of the funerals, Ethel Brunner's bureau had been plundered. Now once may have been chance, twice a coincidence, but three times was a definite pattern, not that the police took much notice and one has to conclude that they were either outrageously incompetent, or under orders not to rock the proverbial boat. Frankly, they didn't have a clue and they were more inclined to downgrade the second burglary as an unsolved minor incident. In doing so they abjectly failed to correlate the latest incident with what may have been two extremely relevant factors.

A few days before the second burglary several newspapers had reported the formal granting of probate on her parents' estates to Princess Shelagh, and that she intended to immediately dispose of Green Cottage. Could this have been the spark for a last desperate search of private papers?

The other, more beguiling element, was the date. The second burglary occurred during the night of Friday March 18 and Saturday March 19, 1927, i.e. within a few hours of the very first meeting of I.C.I. shareholders, a statutory general meeting held in London's Winchester House. Now that was a coincidence!

*****

Years ago, during research for my original book, I interviewed the distinguished science-fiction writer, the late John Brunner, Roscoe and Ethel's grandson. His father was Anthony 'Tony' Brunner, his uncle Patrick Brunner and his aunt, Princess Shelagh. By nature John Brunner seldom looked back. A brusque character his roots and his ancestry held little appeal and he insisted he knew very little about the tragedy. 'I was told only the briefest of details by my father. It was a family scandal not really to be discussed. There may have been something with Sir Alfred Mond, but all I know of him was that it was said that from his deathbed, his father, Ludwig Mond, cursed him. The Brunner and Mond families had been close, but they grew seriously apart in the next generation.'

Strangely, given that John Brunner was only furnished with the 'briefest of details' about his grandparents' deaths, he had been told of the burglary at Green Cottage on the night of the funerals, but not the second break-in at the time of I.C.I.'s first statutory meeting: 'I have heard the story about the burglary on the night of the funerals – it was said they were looking for a second will which my grandfather may have written.'

This was implausible because if Roscoe Brunner had, indeed, prepared a new will it is unlikely he would have kept it at Green Cottage and, besides, who beyond the immediate family would have been interested? For the record, Roscoe and Ethel Brunner's wills were drawn up and retained by the Cheshire firm of solicitors James H.Wadsworth, Ethel's will dated November 28, 1924, and Roscoe's January 30, 1925.

John Brunner's grandparents died years before he was born but in the family his grandmother, Ethel, was always regarded as a 'forceful character' and, much to her amusement, had once been mistaken for the Queen of Romania. Then there was Princess Shelagh, 'Aunt

Shelagh' who was well-remembered by John Brunner: 'When Aunt Shelagh married the Prince it was a morganatic marriage in Liechtenstein. The Prince was definitely a playboy and on the night of their wedding at Claridge's he left her to flirt with an actress. It was a loveless marriage and they soon divorced. Aunt Shelagh eventually remarried, to an Austrian/Hungarian citizen who came to be interred on the Isle of Man during the Second World War.'

John Brunner was unable to add anything further, whereas his sister, Verena Thornton, was rather more forthcoming. Seldom had she heard the tragedy discussed in detail, but it was felt within the family that Roscoe had accidentally shot her grandmother whilst attempting to take his own life: 'The only additional information I have came from my mother, but her interest was not in the event itself, rather on the effect it had on my father. What my mother did tell me was that there was a story about my grandfather covering up for someone within the company, someone who had been involved in underhand dealings...'

The tragedy, she added, was a taboo subject, emphatically not to be discussed outside of the family, an edict extended to the author W.J.Reader during his research into I.C.I.'s official history: 'Dr Reader contacted my mother for information about the tragedy, but when my Aunt Elaine (Patrick Brunner's widow) heard about it, she put her foot down. It seems that at such a late date there are (or were) people around who felt the matter was too sensitive for publication.'

Interestingly, Reader, who died in 1990, was fascinated by the Brunner deaths and in 2007, Dr Peter Morris, Head of Research at the London Science Museum, remarked: 'I remember Reader giving a paper on the tragic fall and suicide of Roscoe Brunner. He intended to write a novel on these events and it was clear he relished the dramatic and human elements of the prelude to the creation of I.C.I..'

Chapter 23

CHRONOLOGY OF EVENTS 1922 - 1927

November 15, 1922
General Election – Conservatives victory.
Sir Alfred Mond wins Swansea West, but is out of Ministerial office.

January 5, 1923
Sir Alfred Mond rejoins Brunner Mond board.

March 2, 1923
Brunner Mond board recognises 'special services' of Sir Alfred Mond.

June 1923
Brunner Mond & Company celebrates Golden Jubilee.

September 1923
Sir Alfred Mond joins board of Brunner Mond's Synthetic & Ammonia Nitrates Ltd, Billingham.

December 6, 1923
Sir Alfred Mond suffers General Election defeat in Swansea West.

January/February 1924
Sir Alfred Mond holidays in India with Viceroy, Lord Reading.

March 1, 1924
Roscoe Brunner sends personal letter to Lever Bros.

June 5, 1924
Brunner Mond board sets up, under Roscoe Brunner, director committee to deal with Lever writ. Roscoe Brunner re-elected company chairman.

August 14, 1924
Sir Alfred Mond wins Camarthen by-election.

January 14, 1925
Shelagh Brunner's marriage to Prince Ferdinand of Liechtenstein.

July, 1925
Roscoe Brunner permitted leave of absence from Brunner Mond due to illness, shingles.

September 12, 1925
Ethel Brunner hosts Warrington Conservative Association Garden Party for 1,500 at Belmont Hall.

September, 1925
Brunner Mond workers' annual outing to Blackpool.
Roscoe Brunner declares himself
'absolutely recovered – very fit, indeed'.
November 5, 1925
Brunner Mond board agrees £1 million settlement with Lever Bros.
Roscoe Brunner in the chair.
January, 1926
January, 1926 Sir Alfred Mond quits Liberal Party,
March 4, 1926
Brunner Mond board accepts Roscoe Brunner's offer of resignation.
Sir Alfred Mond appointed interim chairman.
April 14, 1926
Roscoe Brunner attends Brunner Mond board meeting, London.
Reappointed onto the board's Finance & Policy Committee.
April 29, 1926
Brunner Mond board appoints Sir Alfred Mond chairman.
May 8, 1926
Birth of Prince Ferdinand and Princess Shelagh's son.
May 1926
Brunner Mond Annual Meeting, Liverpool.
May/June 1926
Roscoe & Ethel Brunner acquire Roehampton Court.
July - September, 1926
Roscoe Brunner attends Brunner Mond board meetings, London.
October 12, 1926
RMS Aquitania docks Southampton.
October 19, 1926
Brunner Mond special board meeting, London
to discuss merger proposals.
October 21, 1926
Announcement of 'proposed fusion' of four chemical companies.
October 23, 1926
Sir Alfred Mond MP to be chairman of I.C.I..
October 25, 1926
Four Brunner Mond directors named to serve on the board of I.C.I..
October 26/27, 1926
Roscoe Brunner visits Cheshire, chairs meeting at Winnington.
Guest speaker at Northwich Conservatives' dinner.

October 28, 1926
Sir Jack Brunner announces unable to accept Liberal nomination for Northwich due to 'great changes' at Brunner Mond.
October 29, 1926
Roscoe Brunner spends weekend with his wife at Green Cottage.
November 1, 1926
I.C.I. prospectus released with non-executive director appointees.
November 2, 1926
National newspapers announce composition of ICI board.
Ethel Brunner visits Daily Herald and Daily Telegraph.
Remonstrates at London home of Sir Alfred Mond.
November 3, 1926
Ethel Brunner calls at Financial News.
Bodies of Roscoe and Ethel Brunner discovered at Green Cottage.
November 4, 1926
Sir Jack Brunner attributes tragedy to Ethel Brunner's newspaper visits and Roscoe Brunner's ill-health.
November 5, 1926
Sensational newspaper coverage of Brunner tragedy.
Sir Alfred Mond meets with Westminster Coroner.
November 6-7, 1926
Global news coverage of Brunner tragedy.
November 8, 1926
Inquest, Wandsworth Baths. Verdicts: 'Murder' – Ethel Brunner, 'Suicide whilst of unsound mind' – Roscoe Brunner.
November 9, 1926
Funerals of Roscoe and Ethel Brunner.
Burglary at Green Cottage.
Sir Alfred Mond dispatches 'letter of thanks' to
Metropolitan Police Commissioner.
November, 1926
Brunner case file classified by Metropolitan Police
under 'Hundred Years' rule.
December 7, 1926
I.C.I. formally incorporated with authorized capital of £65 million.
March 19/20, 1927
ICI Statutory General Meeting, Winchester House, London.
Second burglary at Green Cottage.

Chapter 24

METROPOLITAN Police records, newspaper reports, Brunner family interviews and, crucially, the last surviving witness, Bella Hockenhull (née Scott), have provided the bulk of research. Prior to original publication, in 2003, I also made contact with the 4th Baron Melchett who declined to comment, but on revisiting the case almost two decades later, I am more convinced than ever that I.C.I., Britain's foremost industrial empire of the 20th century, was built on a cover-up orchestrated by the 1st Baron Melchett, Sir Alfred Mond, who went to extraordinary lengths to protect the merger and his own reputation.

The Brunner deaths were a sensation without parallel and yet the doubts tumble from a hollow investigation. Doubts expressed by servants, by Haydn Brown, by the journalist William Underhill, by common workers at Brunner Mond. Their opinions counted for nothing. The stakes were too high when Sir Alfred Mond intervened with the coroner to deflect rampant Press speculation away from the merger which, like a giant blue whale, had risen unexpectedly from the depths of the Atlantic. Someone's reputation had to be sacrificed and Mond, ruthlessly ambitious, made sure it wasn't going to be his, or Roscoe Brunner's for that matter – Brunner was far too close to the I.C.I. merger for comfort.

In the final reckoning there wasn't a conspiracy to commit murder, but there was certainly a conspiracy to conceal the truth and, perhaps, it went as far as ensuring the Brunner file was committed to the 'Hundred Years' secrecy archives. I am not suggesting the coroner and the police were deliberately party to a cover-up, rather they were pressured and overawed, 'Yes sir, No sir', by Mond who was a huge political and industrial figure. As to the inquest, the media-obsessed coroner simply endorsed the most rational and logical explanation. He failed to evaluate the facts objectively and, as a result, 'fairness and balance', the basic tenet of any inquest, then or now, flew out of the window. The verdicts were crudely obvious on the evidence permitted, but the wider ramifications were ignored: Mond's return to the Brunner Mond board, betrayal and the cataclysmic Lever affair, Roscoe Brunner's health, his move to London, the revolver, and, most of all, the formation of I.C.I..

Central to the official investigation was Brunner's health and his wife's innocuous round of calls to the newspapers, but neither was properly considered. Brunner may not have been in the most robust of heath, but he was hardly suicidal and there wasn't a shred of evidence to show he shot Ethel because she had already visited the newspapers. It was pure supposition and only those suffering from acute tunnel vision would dismiss as irrelevant the significance of the hat and coat at the moment of death, or why Brunner carried a loaded revolver to Green Cottage when, plainly, he was unaware of what she had been up to in Fleet Street.

There were too many puzzling questions, too many witnesses told to shut up, and it was understandable that some friends and servants believed the inquest was a smokescreen reeking of self-interest, primarily the self-interest of Sir Alfred Mond, Sir Jack Brunner and the coroner Ingleby Oddie, although for good measure one could throw in the police who conducted an investigation that was worse than useless, almost over and done with before it began, and then, hide-bound by a ridiculous timeframe, were expected to appear competent. All had their own reasons for wanting a deeply embarrassing affair archived and forgotten, but Mond, a shrewd political opportunist, certainly had the most to lose.

The inquest achieved its objective, to assuage the family's sorrow, and, to the great relief of Sir Alfred Mond and Sir Jack Brunner, snatch the sting of scandal from the heart of the I.C.I. merger. The public's thirst for answers was generally satisfied and there the matter might have rested had it not been for the two audacious burglaries at Green Cottage. Ripe with intrigue this aspect still hangs tantalisingly by a gossamer thread of speculation rather than sturdy fibres of fact, but it takes an enormous leap of faith to accept the police notion that the two break-ins, four months apart and replicas in their execution, were not connected with the Brunner deaths. Common burglars, professional or amateur, do not break into a property to target a single room and, in the process, ignore rich pickings.

Something far more sinister was going on and the evidence points to the culprits searching for documents that Ethel Brunner intended for the newspapers. Her earlier visits to Fleet Street had been little more than an opening gambit, to pave the way for Roscoe himself to very publicly denounce Mond. When he point-blank refused he was met with a barrage of withering scorn as Ethel impulsively reached for her hat and coat, the fuse for murder, just as the psychiatrist Haydn Brown had said: 'Of late Mr Brunner had no power to persuade her on any point whatsoever; his expostulations only aroused her determination to be energetic all the more'.

It is impossible to know for sure what Ethel Brunner planned to reveal, but she was a woman scorned and in the midst of the all-pervading I.C.I. merger there was no-one else in the frame for her wrath other than Sir Alfred Mond. He had polarised opinion during the war and his role may have been duplicitous in Brunner Mond's tawdry and secretive Lever affair, but these were matters from years earlier, whereas still doing the rounds was the storm over Billingham and accusations that a government minister had abused his position to favour Brunner Mond. If this was true, and Ethel Brunner possessed incriminating proof, as she may have intimated during her outburst on Mond's doorstep, it would have been dynamite to the Mond-McGowan axis and the entire I.C.I. merger. Nothing came to light during the police investigation, or in Sir Jack Brunner's initial scrutiny of private papers, but that isn't to say documents had not existed. The two burglaries starkly appear to have had a single objective, to make doubly sure there was nothing to threaten the merger. Equally, we cannot dismiss the possibility that both burglaries were conducted at Mond's behest as, after all, absence of evidence is not always evidence of absence.

I believe Roscoe Brunner murdered his wife and destroyed the documents in order to protect from an almighty scandal the good name and reputation of Brunner Mond. In doing so, he saved the colossus that was to become I.C.I. and, perhaps he did die a martyr to duty, but for all that he was a murderer and, unquestionably, the innocent, much maligned victim was Ethel Brunner. In the final analysis, one fact stands out, and it is absolutely irrefutable. The Brunner deaths would never have happened had it not been for the frenzy to create I.C.I..

The last word must go to none other than Winston Churchill. It is a reference that comes unsubstantiated, but from a reliable source. In 1940, Sir Harry McGowan, who had succeeded Mond as chairman of I.C.I., was working closely with the wartime government and was perceived to be a noisy, bullying type. To rein him in, Churchill threatened to make public the truth about the Brunner deaths!

Epilogue

FROM almost penniless beginnings and through Victorian entrepreneurial doggedness the Brunners and Monds emerged to become two of Britain's most remarkable families. Their wealth carried them to the highest echelons of society and political power; they married into Royalty, made benefactions of unimaginable proportions and touched on the lives of millions. The two families were – and still are – indebted to the huge success of the Brunner Mond business and the I.C.I. merger, but there was a price to pay. Within four years of the 1926 tragedy, Sir John Brunner and Sir Alfred Mond were both dead.

BRUNNER FAMILY
Sir John Tomlinson Brunner, 1st Bart. (1842-1919)
Co-founder of Brunner Mond. Member of Parliament for Northwich 1885-1886, 1887-1910. Chairman of Brunner Mond & Co Ltd 1891-1918, succeeded by his son, Roscoe Brunner. In 1895 Sir John Brunner was created a Baronet. A Deputy Lieutenant of Lancashire and Pro Chancellor of the University of Liverpool he was a generous benefactor and subscribed £25,000 towards construction of the Runcorn and Widnes Transporter Bridge. Twice married he had eight children, John Fowler Leece Brunner (2nd Bart.), Grace, Sydney, Harold Roscoe, Mabel Alicia, Hilda, Maud Mary, Ethel Jane (Effie).

Sir John Fowler Leece Brunner, 2nd Bart. (1865-1929)
Eldest son (Jack) of Sir John Tomlinson Brunner, 1st Bart. Married Lucy Marianne Vaughan Morgan. MP Leigh Division (Lancashire) 1906-10;

Northwich 1910-18; Southport 1923-24. Director of Brunner Mond, Director of Imperial Chemical Industries 1926-1927. Daughter Joyce Morgan Brunner married Sir William Arthur Worsley. In 1961 Sir John's granddaughter, Katharine Lucy Mary Worsley, married King George V's grandson Prince Edward and became H.R.H. The Duchess of Kent.

Sir Felix John Morgan Brunner, 3rd Bart. (1897-1982)

Son of Sir John Fowler Leece Brunner, 2nd Bart. Educated Cheltenham, Oxford. Wartime service as 1st Lieutenant Royal Field Artillery. Stood for Liberals in Hulme, Chippenham and Northwich but never elected to Parliament. Married, 1926, Elizabeth Irving, granddaughter of English stage actor Sir Henry Irving. In 1937 Sir Felix and Lady Brunner purchased Greys Court, Oxfordshire and in 1969 donated the property to the National Trust. Lady Brunner was Chairman of the National Federation of Women's Institutes 1951-1956 and Founder, in 1955, of Keep Britain Tidy Group. Son John Henry Kilian Brunner is the 4th Bart.

Roscoe Brunner (1871-1926)

Educated Cheltenham, Cambridge. Admitted to Inner Temple to practice as a barrister. Director Brunner Mond & Co. 1901-1926, Chairman Brunner Mond & Co. 1918 - 1925. Deputy Lieutenant of Cheshire, Justice of the Peace. Married in 1898 Ethel Houston, daughter of Arthur Houston KC.

Anthony Brunner (1901-1970)

Eldest son of Roscoe and Ethel Brunner. Christened Egbert Sydney Houston Brunner but changed name by deed poll in 1919 – a 'bonny baby' he always known within the family as 'Tony Lumpkin' and 'Tony' stuck. Educated Cheltenham, Cambridge. 2nd Lieut. Royal Artillery (Territorial Army) suffered serious financial losses in Wall Street crash and later badly injured playing polo. Married 1934, Phyllis Ivy (Felicity) Whittaker. Three children, (i) John Kilian Houston Brunner (1934-1995), science fiction author, (ii) Verena Hilda May (1937-2000) married Edward William Thornton, (iii) Jennifer Margaret Felicity married John Marchant.

Shelagh Salome Houston Brunner (1902-1983)

Daughter of Roscoe and Ethel Brunner, married, 1925, Prince Ferdinand Aloys Andreas Joseph Anton Maria of Liechtenstein (1901-1981). Children Christopher Richard Francis von Rietberg and Ethel Elisabeth, Olga, Mary von Rietberg (born Soos Castle, Austria, September 1928). Marriage dissolved 1934, ecclesiastically annulled 1939 'not having met the lawful requirements of the ruling dynasty of Liechtenstein'. Shelagh granted name and title Countess von Rietberg. Secondly married, 1934, Georg Otto Suppancic. Divorced 1952. Prince Ferdinand married secondly in Stockholm, 1940, Brita Christina Nordenskold. Divorced 1948. Married thirdly, in Suffolk County, New York 1950, Dorothy Haidel. Married fourthly, in Sucy-en-Brie, 1968, Nadine Georgette Maria Ansay.

Princess Shelagh and Prince Ferdinand's son Christopher (1926-2005) took title Count Christopher von Rietberg. Served with 15th/19th Hussars. Married 1955, Kathleen Hamilton, of Orangeberg, New York. Children: Gabrielle Catherine (b. 1957) and Mark Andreas (b.1959).

Ethel Elisabeth Olga Mary, the daughter of Princess Shelagh and Prince Ferdinand, came to be titled Countess von Rietberg, married, 1953, Klaus Bruno von Brehm – divorced 1961. Secondly married, 1968, Richard Onslow.

Patrick Brunner (1908-1966)

Oswald Patrick O'Brien Brunner, third child of Roscoe and Ethel Brunner. Educated Cheltenham, Cambridge. Film producer and Wing Commander RAF Volunteer Reserve. Allegedly assisted in the drafting of Churchill's wartime speeches. Married, 1933, London/New York dancer Mary Elaine Howlett, daughter of Richard Howlett, Superintendent of the King's Wardrobe and official Cocker of the King's Gun. Queen Mary was Mary Elaine's godmother. The Brunner - Howlett marriage ceremony took place in the Chapel Royal, St James's Palace, by permission of King George V. During the Second World War, Mary Elaine was a member of Oxford Police and Observer Corps, reportedly spotting enemy aircraft from an open-topped MG. One daughter, Mary Elizabeth April Brunner, born 1936. Her godmother was also Queen Mary.

MOND FAMILY
Dr Ludwig Mond (1839-1909)

Co-founder of Brunner Mond. Also formed Mond Nickel Co with mines in Canada and works near to Swansea. President of the Society of General Chemical Industry, Member of the Royal Society. In his later years he built up a collection of old master paintings and the greater proportion of these he bequeathed to the National Gallery. Married Frida Lowenthal, Cologne 1866. His estate was valued at £1 million. Two sons, Robert and Alfred. Robert, a chemist and archaeologist, was knighted in 1932.

Sir Alfred Mond, Baron Melchett (1868-1930)

Sir Alfred Mond's peerage materialized in June 1928, not the coveted Viscountcy, but a Barony. He took the title Baron Melchett of Landford (the extra 't' to the name of Melchet Court was apparently a whim). His coat of arms included a crescent moon in acknowledgement of the Mond family name – the crescent moon was also the emblem of Brunner Mond & Co. Ltd. In Parliament for over twenty-two years, represented Chester, Swansea West and Carmarthen. President of the Empire Economic Union, President of the World Power Conference and Fellow of the Royal Society. Honorary degrees from Oxford, Paris and other universities.

In latter years championed for the free state of Israel and was first President of the Technion (now the Israel National Museum of Science, Technology and Space) founded in 1924 with the support of Albert Einstein. Chairman of the Economic Board for Palestine, President of British Zionist Foundation and founded, in the Sharon region, town of Tel Mond. His statue now dominates the town and his former home serves as a museum, the 'House of the Lord'. Tel Aviv and other Israeli cities have roads named 'Melchett Street'.

Died aged 62, four years after founding of I.C.I.. Left estate exceeding £1 million. Funeral rites conducted at Finchley and I.C.I. factories throughout the world ceased work whilst he was laid to rest. The following day a memorial service was held, attended by over 1,000 employees, colleagues, friends and family. Not a single member of the Brunner family appears to have been present.

Lord Melchett's statue in Tel Mond.

Violet Mond, Baroness Melchett (1867-1945)

Sir Alfred Mond's wife, a political hostess and worker, was said to have used her influence with David Lloyd George to secure her husband's appointment to ministerial office in 1916. Appointed Dame Commander of the British Empire in 1920. Heavily involved in infant welfare, chairing the Violet Melchett Centre, a combined infant welfare centre, day nursery and mothers' home in Chelsea, originally financed by husband.

Henry Mond, 2nd Baron Melchett (1898-1949)

The only son of Alfred and Violet Mond. Deputy Chairman of I.C.I. 1940-47. Served as MP for Isle of Ely 1923-24 and Liverpool East Toxteth 1929-30. Married Amy Gwen Wilson in 1920. Eldest son, Derek, killed in flying accident whilst serving with the Royal Naval Reserves in 1945.

Eva Mond, Marchioness of Reading (1895-1973)

Sir Alfred Mond's daughter. Became Marchioness of Reading through marriage to Gerald Isaacs, the 2nd Marquess of Reading. She was Vice President of the World Jewish Congress and President of its British section. To mark her worldwide promotion of Jewish rights she was awarded an honorary fellowship at the Hebrew University of Jerusalem.

Julian Mond 3rd Baron Melchett (1925-1973)

Son of Henry Mond, 2nd Baron Melchett. Educated Eton, joined Fleet Air Arm in 1942, served on Russian convoys. A leading businessman he chaired government committee to plan nationalization of British Steel industry and was effectively chairman of British Steel Corporation.

Peter Henry Mond 4th Baron Melchett

Born 1948. Educated Eton and Cambridge. Parliamentary Under-Secretary of State in Labour's Department of Industry. In 1976 under James Callaghan's premiership was appointed Minister of State at the Northern Ireland Office. Served as President of the Ramblers' Association 1981-84, Executive Director of Greenpeace 1989-2000. Appointed Director of the Soil Association in 2002.

OTHERS
John Gibb Nicholson

Joined board of Brunner Mond 1919 and part of informal triumvirate with Roscoe Brunner and James Herbert Gold. Untarnished by Lever affair he was appointed a member of the inaugural board of I.C.I.. Later Deputy Chairman of I.C.I., knighted 1944.

Sir Harry Duncan McGowan, Baron McGowan (1874-1961)

Founded I.C.I. with Sir Alfred Mond. President 1926-1930, Chairman and Managing Director 1930-1937, Chairman 1937-1950. Raised to Peerage 1937 as Baron McGowan of Ardeer in the County of Ayr.

Rufus Daniel Isaacs, Marquess of Reading (1860-1935)

Viceroy and Governor General of India, 1921-26. One of original directors of I.C.I. and later became President. Secretary of State for Foreign Affairs, 1931, Lord Warden of Cinque Ports, 1934.

Lord Ashfield (1874-1948)

MP Ashton under Lyne 1916-20. President of the Board of Trade 1916-19. Government director, chairman of British Dyestuffs Corporation.

Samuel Ingleby Oddie (1869-1945)

Westminster Coroner. Presided at the inquest into the deaths of Roscoe and Ethel Brunner. Presided,1931, at inquest into victims of R101 airship disaster. Retired 1939 when it was said his combination of wide practical experience, both of law and medicine, had made him an excellent coroner. Obituary noted his 'clarity and strength of mind'. Conducted over 20,000 inquests.

Det Insp. Albert Eve

Lead officer into the deaths of Roscoe and Ethel Brunner. Born Bishopsgate, London 1881. Joined Metropolitan Police 1902 and completed 27 years' service. Retired with 'excellent record' in June 1929.

IMPERIAL CHEMICAL INDUSTRIES (I.C.I.)

I.C.I. commenced with 33,000 employees. Products included chemicals, explosives and accessories, fertilisers, insecticides, dyestuffs, domestic chemicals, leathercloth, printing, sporting ammunition and paints. Seventy years later it had 64,000 employees worldwide and in excess of 8,000 products. By 2006 annual revenue topped £4.8 billion. In 1991 the Mid Cheshire soda ash sector was incorporated into a separate company that went on to be acquired by TATA Chemicals Limited, of India. I.C.I. itself moved away from bulk chemicals and, eventually, the remaining business was acquired by the Dutch company AkzoNobel. The price paid: £8 billion.

THE BRUNNER INVESTMENT TRUST

In 1927, with rewards from the merging of Brunner Mond into I.C.I., the Brunner family established an Investment Trust. Sir Felix Brunner 3rd Bart. served as Chairman of the Trust 1927-1972. Latest available accounts reveal Brunner Investment Trust assets amount to over £500 million (2022).

Sources

The First Fifty Years of Brunner Mond & Company
The Brunner Papers - Sidney Jones Library, University of Liverpool
A History of the Alkali Division, A.S.Irvine
A History of Winnington Hall, A.S.Irvine
The Life of Ludwig Mond, J.M.Cohen
The Mond Legacy, Jean Goodman
Sir John Brunner, Radical Plutocrat, 1842-1919, Stephen E.Koss
A Hundred Years of Alkali in Cheshire, W.F.L.Dick
I.C.I. The Company That Changed Our Lives, Carol Kennedy
The Chemical Industry's Participation in Industrial Relations, J.K.Bottomley
Imperial Chemical Industries: A History, W.J.Reader
The Awakening Giant, Andrew M.Pettigrew
The History of Unilever, Charles Wilson
Alfred Mond, The First Lord Melchett, Hector Bolitho
In Memory of Alfred Mond Baron Melchett of Landford 1868-1930
I Bought a Newspaper, Claude Morris
Lloyd George - The Goat in the Wilderness, Jonathan Cape
War Memories, David Lloyd George
Tempestuous Journey - Lloyd George: His Life and Times, Frank Owen
The Downfall of the Liberal Party 1914-1935, Trevor Wilson
The Marconi Scandal, Frances Donaldson
Brave New World, Aldous Huxley
Mad For Zion, Colonel J.H.Patterson
White Mischief, James Fox
Memoirs of a London County Coroner, H.R.Oswald
Notable British Trials, edited Geoffrey Clarke
Rufus Isaacs, First Marquess of Reading, Marquess of Reading
Cheshire Leaders, Social and Political, Ernest Gaskell
Ethel Brunner novels: Celia and Her Friends, The Elopement – Celia Intervenes, Celia Once Again, Celia's Fantastic Voyage

Parliamentary Debates (Hansard)
British Newspaper Library
British Newspaper Archives
Public Record Office Kew
General Register Office
Battersea Library
Cheshire Archives & Local Studies

A wide range of newspapers and journals have been consulted including: The Times, Daily Herald, Daily Telegraph, London Evening Standard, Daily Express, Daily Mail, Morning Post, New Witness, Sunday Express, Sunday Pictorial, Sunday Chronicle, News of the World, Weekly Dispatch, Sketch, Financial News, Manchester Guardian, Liverpool Daily Post, Warrington Guardian, Northwich Guardian, Chester Chronicle, Cheshire Observer, Montreal Gazette, Pittsburgh Press, Singapore Free Press.

Acknowledgments

The author's grateful thanks are due to Mike Beddard, Geoff Buchan, John Buckley, John Chesworth, Elaine Hanson, Colin Lynch, Trevor Hearing and, especially, Paul Lavell. Their support has been unstinting on what has been an exceedingly long journey.

To the living give only respect;
To the dead only truth.
— Voltaire